TRIGGER

edited by Robert Klanten, Hendrik Hellige, Michael Mischler

Abuse Industries
aeonflux | autobulb d.care
Andreas Prossliner
Approach & Identity
Bastien Aubry
Bianca Strauch
BOROS
büro destruct
Büro X
Chalet
DED Associates
Dextro
Dirk Rudolph
D. Martijn Oostra
e-boy
Eikes Grafischer Hort
Factor Product
Fons Matthias Hickmann
Formgeber
Function
G
Hell
Hideki Inaba Design
HinderSchlatterFeuz Grafik
i_d büro
Johannes Deutsch
Judith Rüegger & Anna Albisetti
Kai Twellbeck
Kim Hiorthøy
King Cay Lab
KM7
Maja Gusberti
Marc Kappeler
Marok
Martin Woodtli
Mika Mischler
MoM'n'DaD Productions
norm
Pfadfinderei.Mitte
Planet Pixel
Production 13
Ruth Held
Sagmeister Inc.
Speedshop
Stefan Gandl
(Strada
Stylorouge
Surface
Sweden
The Designers Republic
Threshold House
Toursalon
Transport
Tycoon Graphics
United Visions
Weissraum
Wieden & Kennedy/Nike
52 mm

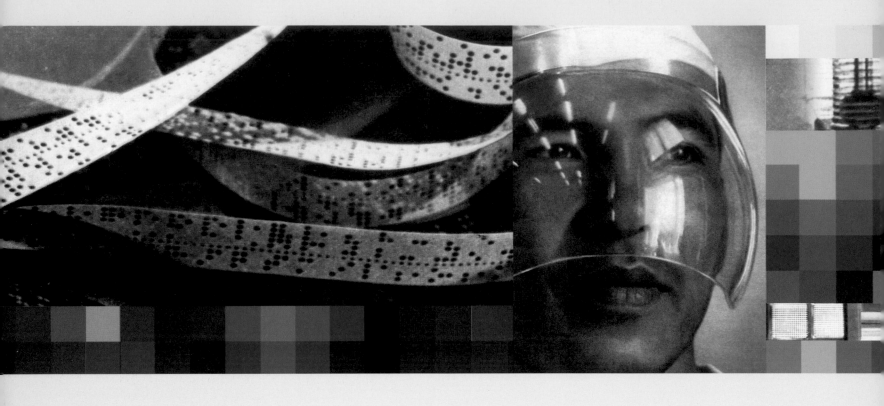

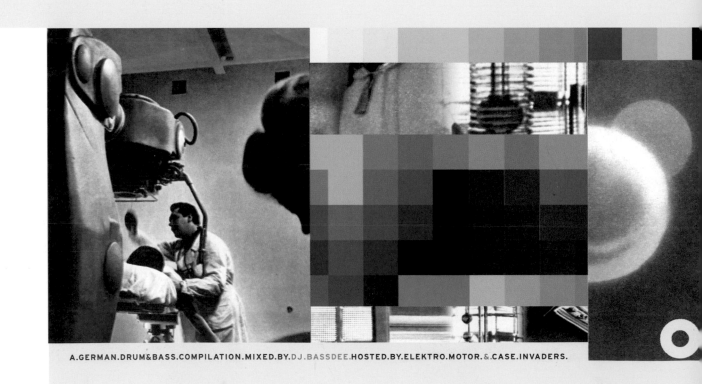

A.GERMAN.DRUM&BASS.COMPILATION.MIXED.BY.DJ.BASSDEE.HOSTED.BY.ELEKTRO.MOTOR.&.CASE.INVADERS.

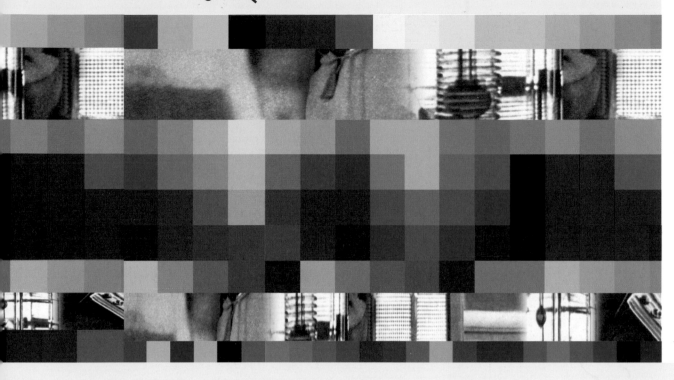

1 FLAMINGO CLUB: Home of the organ sax sound regularly presents Georgie Fame, Tony Knight's Chessmen, Chris Farlowe and the Thunderbirds, Herbie Goins the Night Timers. Tube: Piccadilly or Leicester Sq., walk to 33-37 Wardour St. Coffee bar service.

2 MARQUEE CLUB: Cradle of many famous groups. Hear Spencer Davis, the Who, Steam Packet, Moody Blues, Dedicated Men, Vagabonds, Mark Leeman Five, Yardbirds, Manfred Mann. Tube: Oxford Circus walk to 90 Wardour St. Licensed bar Wednesday folk night. Coffee bar service.

3 100 CLUB: Traditional jazz returning, but hear the Bo Street Runners and Art Woods. Has the Radio Caroline Show Thursdays with pop stars like Ivy League and Tommy Roe guesting. Tube: Oxford Circus or Tottenham Ct. Rd. walk to 100 Oxford St. Buses 7, 8, 23, 25 and 73.

4 BROMEL CLUB: Swinging club with a licensed bar at Bromley Court Hotel. Hear Chris Farlowe, Spencer Davis, Georgie Fame, Graham Bond, Zoot Money, Five Dimensions, Alex Harvey, Vagabonds and many others, mainly Sundays and Wednesdays. Train: Bromley North (SR) and 47 bus to Bromley Hill.

5 STUDIO '51: Folk and Blues here as well as R&B groups like Themselves on Friday sessions, and Sunday afternoons. Tube: Leicester Sq., walk to 10/11 Great Newport Street.

6 THE PLUG HOLE: Everybody goes down the Plughole they say, and as well as record sessions hear the Syndicats resident group Friday. Tube: Tottenham Court Road, and walk to number 32.

7 PONTIAC: New action club with pop art decor. Hear Manfred Mann, the Who, Hollies, Donovan, John Mayall and soon, the Byrds. Regulars are the Boston Dexters, Action, Sidewinders and Classmates. Go to Zeeta House, junc. Upper Richmond Road and Putney High Street. Putney Station (SR) East Putney St. (District line).

8 KLOOKS KLEEK: Ex-jazz club now famed for its R&B. Dig the Mike Cotton Sound, Herbie Goins, John Mayall, Zoot Money, Chris Farlowe, Ronnie Jones and the Blue Jays, Brian Auger, Georgie Fame, Jimmy James, Alex Harvey and Graham Bond. Tuesdays and Thursdays. Licensed bar. West Hampstead. Buses 28, 59A, 159.

9 POP INNE: Otherwise known as The Manor House, hear the Who, Jimmy James and the Vagabonds, Hollies, Spencer Davis, Georgie Fame, Ronnie Jones and many more R&B giants. Licensed bar. Tube: Manor House or buses 127, 159, 179, 149 and 123 to Seven Sisters Road, or bus to Lee High Road, 21.

10 BEXLEY JAZZ CLUB: Raving Sunday night R&B as well as Monday trad, with all top groups like Georgie Fame, Spencer Davis, Zoot Money and local group the contest winning Epitaphs Soul Band. Train to Bexley (SR) and buses 89 and 146, to Black Prince Hotel, on the A2.

11 CLUB NOREIK: Once filmed by "World in Action", top poppers like Tom Jones and Hollies mix with Spencer Davis, Georgie Fame type groups. Tube: Manor House or buses 127, 159, 179, 149 and 123 to Seven Sisters Road, Saturday all-nighters only starting at 11 pm.

12 NEW SCENE CLUB: Featured the Animals, Stones and Fame early days. VIPs are residents. Monday, Tuesday, Thursday, Friday, Saturday and Sat. All-nighter. One min. Piccadilly Tube Stn. Buses to Shaftesbury Avenue, walk to Ham Yard, Gt. Windmill Street.

13 EL PARTIDO: Lewisham's hip joint featuring groups like the Loose Ends, Ronnie Jones, Chris Farlowe and the Epitaphs Soul Band. Lewisham Station (SR) 10 minutes, or train to Sidcup (SR).

14 BLACK CAT: Sessions at this Woolwich club on Tues., Thurs., Fri., Sat., Sun. Top groups like the Honeycombs, Unit Four Plus Two, Graham Bond and Epitaphs Square 75, 122 and 229. Train: Woolwich Arsenal (SR).

15 AUSTRAL: Mod scene for with of faces at Sidcup. Record nights plus Epitaphs Soul Band on Thursdays. Buses 51, 229 and 228 or train to Sidcup (SR).

16 LAST CHANCE SALOON: Another Oxford Street Club near the 100 club. Hear the Loose Ends, Rick n' Beckers and Shevells on Thurs., Fri., Sat and Sun. Coffee bar. Tube: Tottenham Court Road.

17 GOLD HAWK: Home of the Who and now the Action. A mods centre in Gold Hawk Road, Shepherd's Bush. Hear also the Clique, Steam Packet, Georgie Fame, Cliff Bennett, Yardbirds and Animals. Licensed bar. Tube: Goldhawk Road.

18 GLENLYN BALLROOM: Friday and Saturday sessions with Goldie and the Gingerbreads, Majority, Rob Storme, Tony Rivers, and Rockers, 324 bus to Perry Vale, Forest Hill and Forest Hill Station (SR).

19 WHITE LION: In Burnt Oak Broadway, Edgware, hear Quiet Five, Epics, Moody Blues, Georgie Fame and Yardbirds. Licensed bar Sunday sessions. Edgware tube.

20 CAVERN: Underneath Ad Lib in L Place, off L Square. F night, head Action, Equ Syndicats, bar. Tube S Square.

TOP POPS
Figures in brackets are mid-week ratings

1 Yeh, Yeh—Georgie Fame
2 I Feel Fine—Beatles
3 Go Now—Moody Blues
4 Girl Don't Come—Sandie Shaw
5
6 Terry—Twinkle
7 I'm Telling You Now—J. Proby
8 Downtown—Petula Clark
9 Somewhere—P. J. Proby
10 Walk Tall—Val Doonican
11 Terry-Cross The Me...
Carry My Love...

st This   ek Week   TITLE   ARTIST

1   ○ YEH, YEH .... Georgie Fame and the Blue Flames
                                                                              (Columbia)

2   ○ I FEEL FINE .... The Beatles (Parlophone)

guide to the clubs where it's all happening

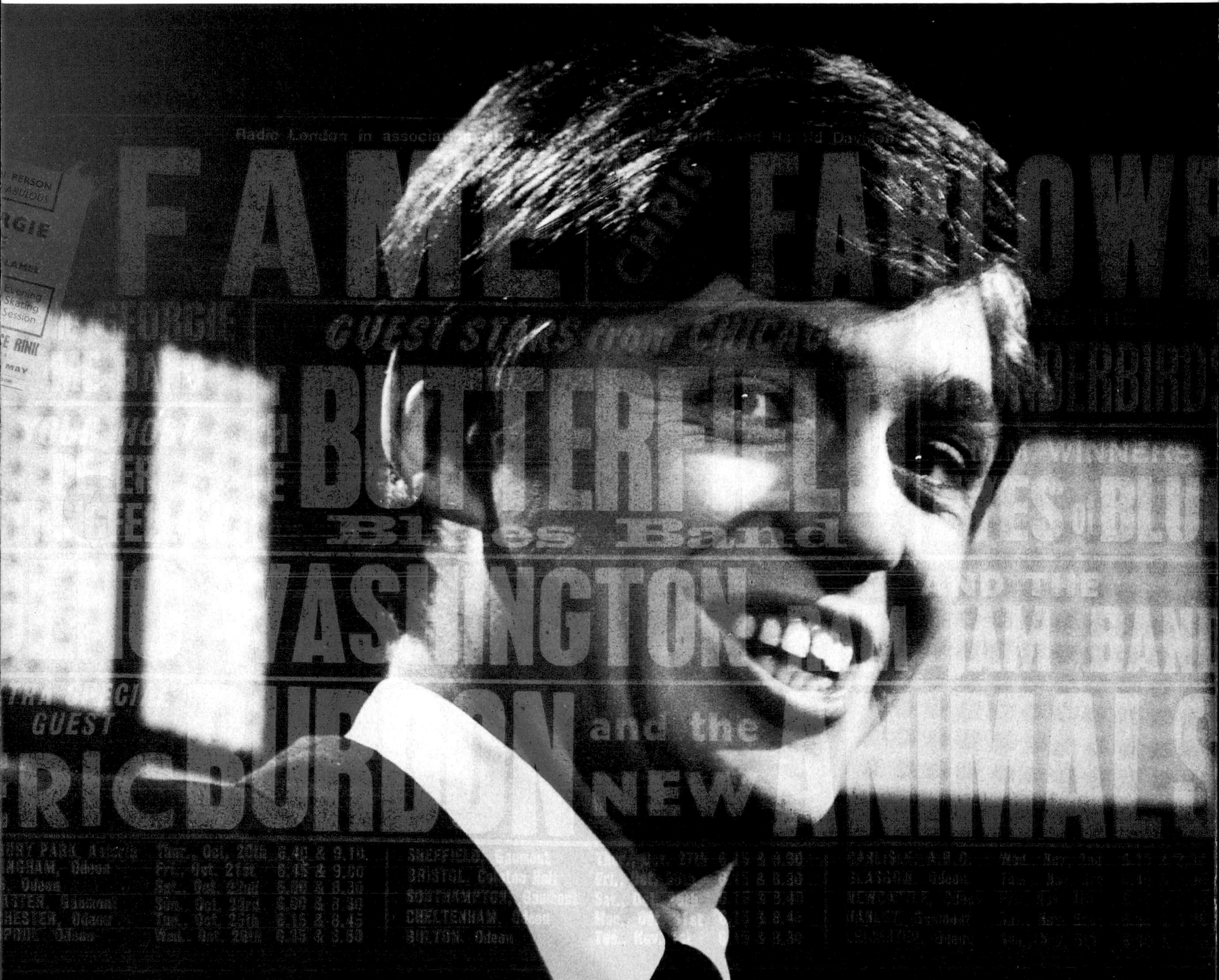

GUEST STARS
GUEST
Evening Skating Session
and the
NEW

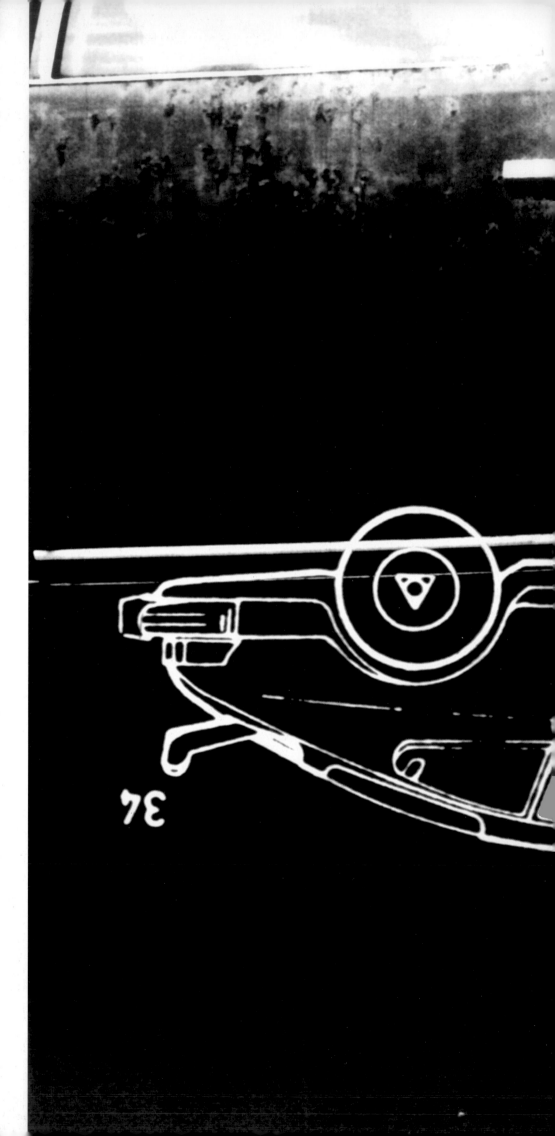

0603'98
1303'98
2003'98
2703'98

style drum&bass · location johannisstrasse20 · jamie white · bassdee :feed :metro :most wanted :x.plorer · hard:edged · continuous club mode · 23.00 · all cap one :flux :bleed · friday:weekly · march(03)'98 · WWF

0198
0201'98
0901'98
1601'98
2301'98
3001'98

style drum&bass · location johannisstrasse20 · jamie white · bassdee :feed :metro :most wanted :x.plorer · hard:edged · continuous club mode · 23.00 · all cap one :flux :bleed · friday:weekly · january(01)'98 · WWF

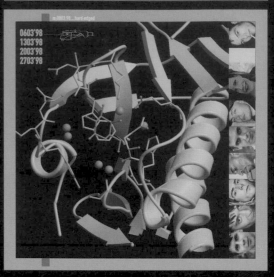

m.0003.98...hard:edged
0603'98
1303'98
2003'98
2703'98

feat.növember.
13(11)reinforced.night.ian|stretch:mc.mg.lounge:dego
20(11)defiant

hard:edged drum'n.bass.continuous.club.mode.(11)98.

m.0002.98...hard:edged
0602'98
1302'98
2002'98
2702'98

0298

**hard:edged.drum'n.bass.
continuous.club.mode.**

**0409'98:1109'98:1809'98:
2509'98:dj:bailey.mc:flux.[metalheadz]**

hard:edged.drum'n.bass.continuous.club.mode.(10)98.

feature:16(10)kemistry|storm(metalheadz)
feat.octöber.

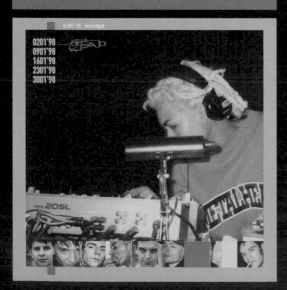

m.0001.98...hard:edged
0201'98
0901'98
1601'98
2301'98
3001'98

040998

hard:edged_07

© SF FONT SERIES; FONTROM #1 16 Original Fonts Available.

[Fontron]

SHIFT FACTORY

SHE DIED IN JUNE

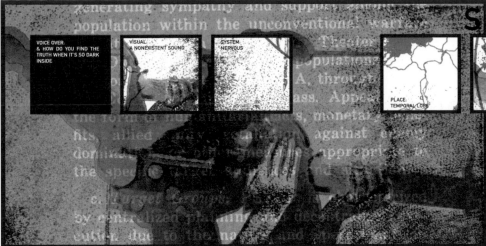

VOICE OVER:
& HOW DO YOU FIND THE
TRUTH WHEN IT'S SO DARK
INSIDE

VISUAL:
A NONEXISTENT SOUND

SYSTEM:
NERVOUS

PLACE:
TEMPORAL LOBE

my name was dragon carrera. my sister, who was about 40, was named jet li carrera. it was my job, along with roseanne and a few others, to bring jet li back from her state of "rest," which was a sort of purgatory because she was supposed to be dead. we went to the tunnel, a damp place where jet li's bed was in darkness, and summoned the watchers of the tunnel. the watchers consisted of two hippies, a young man and woman. the man had long, auburn curly hair pulled back in a ponytail, wearing long draping robes, and he was barefoot despite the wet and muddy ground. i noticed his feet; they were pale and calloused from walking on that cold, wet rock for so many years. so we had to convince him to grant us permission, and when we got it, we heard a noise come from where jet li's bed was, a sort of clicking sound...she was moving. i was afraid, not knowing what would emerge from that darkness. but roseanne was the brave one, and she took me in to see what was there. light slowly illuminated jet li's bed, and she arose, weighing in at about 250 pounds, long grey hair pulled back...quite a hefty woman. she had an unfamiliar, empty look in her eyes and i felt a moment of detatchment. who was she now? could all that darkness change her? we helped her out of the tunnel. then we found ourselves in a playground area that looked a lot like the playground when i went to grade school. jet li started reciting some incantations. as soon as she was done, swift and strong "bullets" of light pierced her chest in 3 places. she was being fired upon by an invisible force, trying to take her back to the purgatory she once came from. roseanne and i watched helplessly. i wondered if she was meant to remain in that dark cave, lifeless and forgotten. jet li got up from the ground, not injured too badly, and we never brought her back because we didn't want to, and she didn't want to go back. we left the playground and the rest i can't remember...it was a dream.

TIME:
IS SOMETHING IMAGINED

death X

9 millimeters equals ten thousand volts.

DEFENSIVE DEFENSIVE+

NO | 646353 7.00PM NO | 46 WASHINGTON PARK

NOVEMBER 25TH

9 millimeters will not equal 10,000 volts if Amnesty International gets it's way by abolishing the death penalty world wide. Will life imprisonment be enough to deter murderers and gang violence? Will that be enough to stop the stray bullets from hitting your child?

You have 10,000 volts. Use them. On November 25th, attend the debate against Amnesty International over the world wide abolition of the death penalty. Every voice must be heard. Remember, 7:00 PM at Washington Park.

A Public Service Announcement brought to you by ACTIVE.

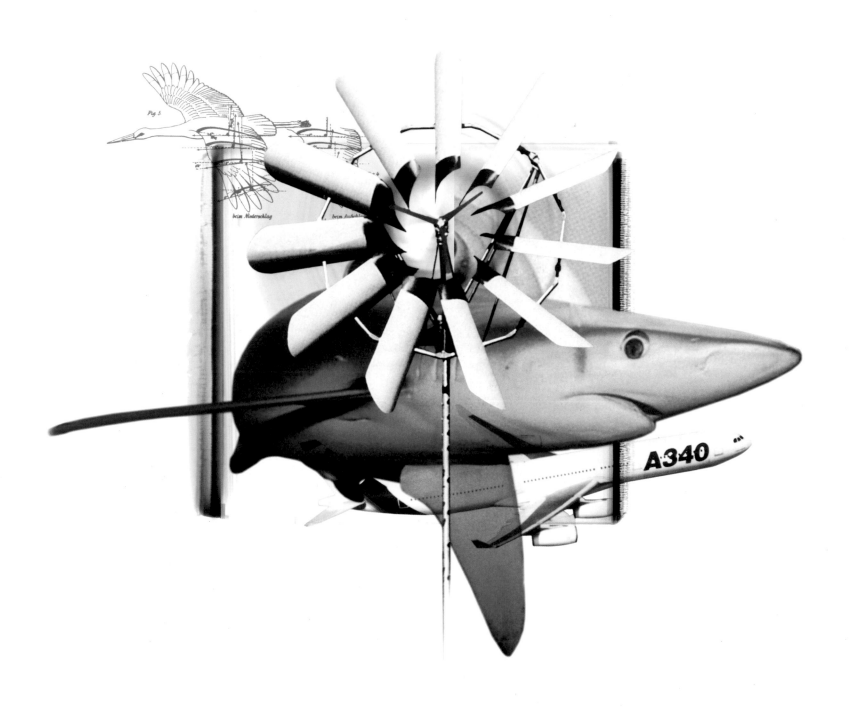

Flügel eines 4 kg schweren Storches.
Maßstab ½ natürlicher Größe.

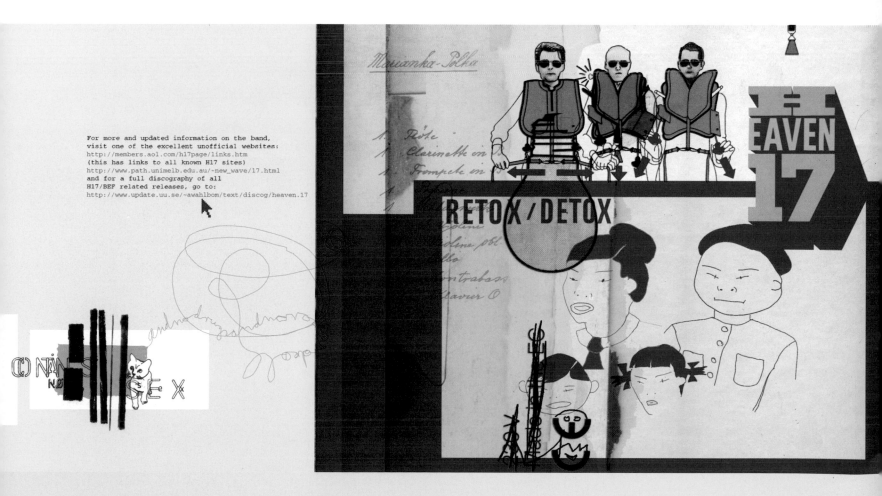

For more and updated information on the band,
visit one of the excellent unofficial websites:
http://members.aol.com/h17page/links.htm
(this has links to all known H17 sites)
http://www.path.unimelb.edu.au/~new_wave/17.html
and for a full discography of all
H17/BEF related releases, go to:
http://www.update.uu.se/~awahlbom/text/discog/heaven.17

peep®

PlayTIPI™

PEEPtheNeueSellWetica! ENJOY.
Exclusive: The first full numeric alphabet in the world
NEUESELLWETICA
FONTalk Live

numericfontservice24hours/day
instantcredit@www.formel1.com

theNeuePayTipi™
theNeueSellwetica-Familycalled PEEP™
peepedbygandl/FORMEL1

peep®
FOR DOWNLOAD™
REPLACE MICRODISK HERE

PlayTIPI™

PEEP theNeueSellWetica! **ENJOY.**

Exclusive: The first full numeric alphabet in the world

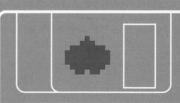

FONTalk Live

numericfontservice24hours/day
instantcredit@www.formel1.com

theNeuePayTipi™
theNeueSellwetica-Familycalled PEEP™
peepedby gandl /FORMEL1

FOR DOWNLOAD™
REPLACE MICRODISK HERE

     the Neue SellWetica™ ©1998 @stefanGandl all rights reserved. @@F1-BERLIN (I♥MY FORMULA!)

FIG↗A

↗A

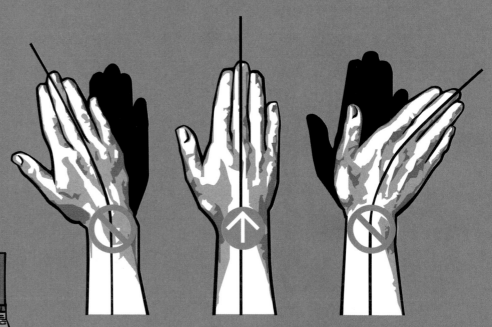

↗B   ↗C   ↗D

FIG↗B↗C↗D

FREEYOURMOUSE™
YOUR MIND WILL FOLLOW

Personnel Recruitment

DESIGNERDOCK®

Headline

*** WIR GEHEN FUER SIE AUF SEH ***

TOUR CODE
1AFASTSTAFF

BOOK. AGT. ID.
DESIGNERDOCK/BERLIN

Copy#1

DOCKEN SIE BEI UNS AN

DATE OF ISSUE
180598

TEL	FAX	ADDRESS	POST CODE
030 691 19 21	030 69 04 19 51	GRIMMSTRASSE 27	10967 BERLIN

ORIGINAL ISSUE

ADDRESS   POST CODE

NAME OF PASSENGER (NOT TRANSFERABLE)

KOMMEN SIE AN BORD!

WIR VERMITTELN KREATIVE AN WERBEAGENTUREN,
DESIGNBUEROS UND UNTERNEHMEN.
DIE AUFNAHME IN UNSERER KARTEI IST KOSTENLOS.
MELDEN SIE SICH BEI UNS UNTER (030) 691 19 21

ISSUED BY
A. DEWHIRST/MR

GRIMMSTRASSE 27 10967
BERLIN

TEL
030 691 19 21

FAX
030 69 04 19 51

Copy#2

SIE SIND AUF SEH?

GRAFIKER*TEXTER*ILLUSTRATOREN*FOTOGRAFEN MIT PROFIL

ADD. INFORMATION
WWW.DESIGNERDOCK.DE

OB FEST ODER FREI/SPEZIALIST ODER PROFI
UND WENN ES SOFORT SEIN MUSS, TAUCHEN UNSERE EINSPRINGER AUF
****

IMPORTANT NOTICE

Slogan

ONLY GOOD STAFF MAKE GOOD STUFF************************************

DO NOT MARK OR STAMP IN THE WHITE AREA ABOVE

DESIGNERDOCK

THIS TICKET IS NOT VALID AND WILL NOT BE ACCEPTED FOR BOARDING UNLESS CONFIRMED THROUGH THE CHANNELS OF A QUALIFIED DESIGNERDOCK CONSULTANT

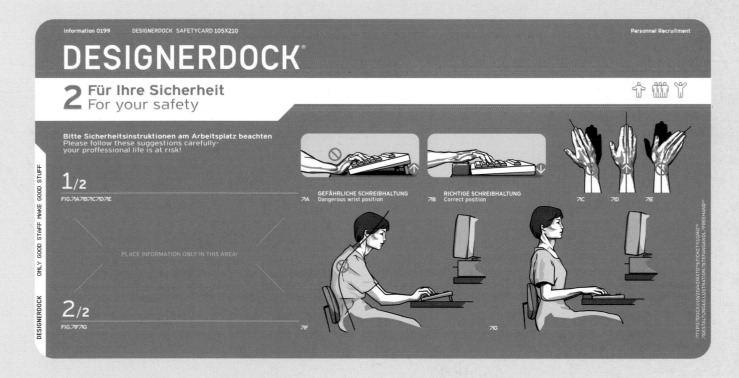

DESIGNERDOCK®

2 Für Ihre Sicherheit
For your safety

Bitte Sicherheitsinstruktionen am Arbeitsplatz beachten
Please follow these suggestions carefully-
your proffessional life is at risk!

1/2
FIG.7|A7|B7|C7|D7|E

PLACE INFORMATION ONLY IN THIS AREA!

2/2
FIG.7|F7|G

GEFÄHRLICHE SCHREIBHALTUNG
Dangerous wrist position   7|A

RICHTIGE SCHREIBHALTUNG
Correct position   7|B

7|C   7|D   7|E

7|F   7|G

ONLY GOOD STAFF MAKE GOOD STUFF

DESIGNERDOCK

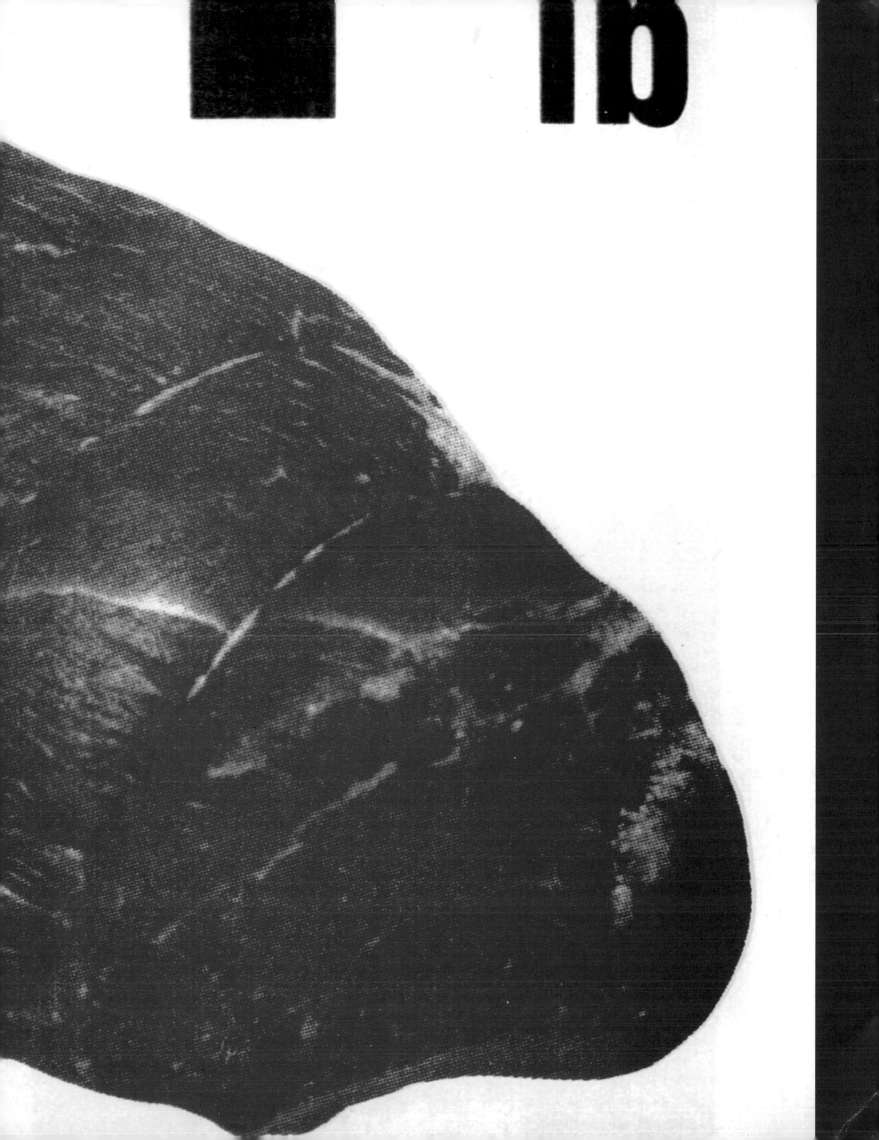

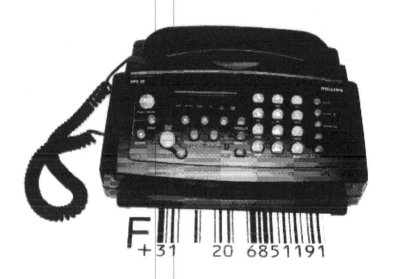

F +31 20 6851191

+31 20 6851191 F

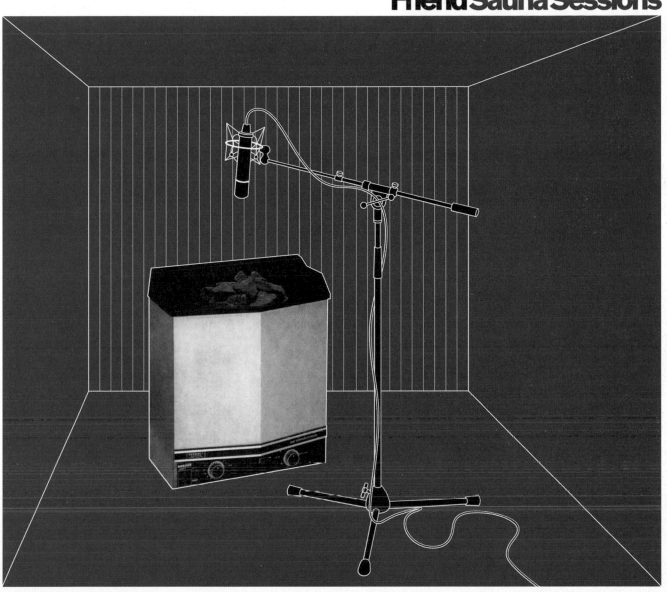

Friend Sauna Sessions

NU BLEV JAG NOJIG

NY SVENSK DRAMATIK AV JOAKIM FORSBERG URPREMIÄR 980129. Natteater med bar fredag och lördag 21:30

Stockholms Improvisationsteater Sigtunagatan 12, T-Bana S:t Eriksplan. Email: info@impro.a.se Internet: www.impro.a.se BILJETTER & INFO: 08 / 30 62 42

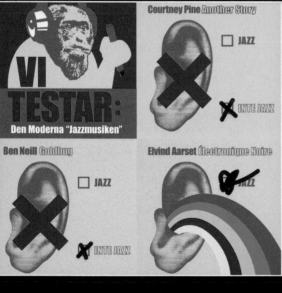

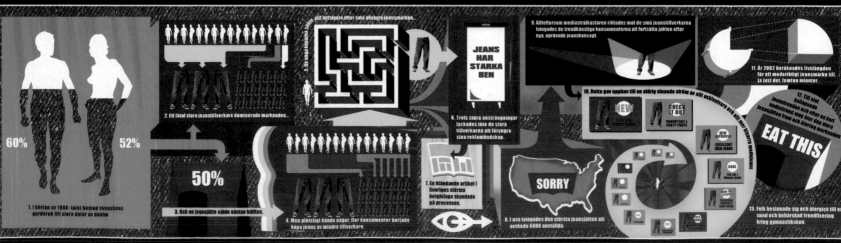

SNUT

"En Kriminellt Improviserad Akt" • Premiär 24/9

 Stockholms Improvisationsteater
Torsdag – Lördag kl.19.00 • Sigtunagatan 12, T - Odenplan

Biljetter och information
08-30 62 42
www.impro.a.se

Biljetter och information
08-30 62 42
www.impro.a.se

Harry Thürk
Das letzte Aloha
DIE
Delikte Indizien Ermittlungen

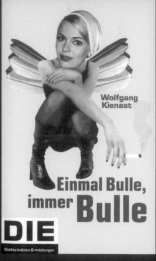

Wolfgang Kienast
Einmal Bulle, immer Bulle
DIE
Delikte Indizien Ermittlungen

Gerhard J. Rekel
DIE
Delikte Indizien Ermittlungen

Jan Flieger
Im Höllenfeuer stirbt man langsam
DIE
Delikte Indizien Ermittlungen

Horst Bastian
Nicht jeden Tag ist Beerdigung
DIE
Delikte Indizien Ermittlungen

Mord light oder Es muß nicht immer Totschlag sein
DIE
Delikte Indizien Ermittlungen

Roberto Ampuero
Bolero in Havanna
DIE
Delikte Indizien Ermittlungen

Frank Goyke und Torsten Schulz
Daniels Strafe
DIE
Delikte Indizien Ermittlungen

MORD für MORD
Max Adam
DIE
Delikte Indizien Ermittlungen

Joachim Wohlgemuth
Auf halbem Weg zum Glück
DIE
Delikte Indizien Ermittlungen

Gerhard Johann
Seitensprung ins nasse Grab
DIE
Delikte Indizien Ermittlungen

Mord total
Gerhard Neumann
DIE

Sangers Fluch
Peter Schrenk
DIE
Delikte Indizien Ermittlungen

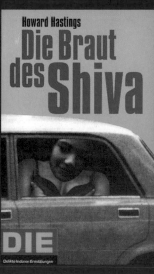

Howard Hastings
Die Braut des Shiva
DIE
Delikte Indizien Ermittlungen

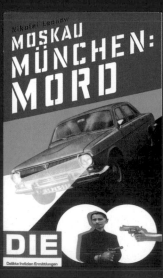

Nikolai Leonow
MOSKAU MÜNCHEN: MORD
DIE
Delikte Indizien Ermittlungen

Harry Thürk
Schwarze Blüte - sanfter Tod
DIE
Delikte Indizien Ermittlungen

gas-

FREE 1998. A&F CO-ORDINATOR JAPAN CO.,LTD

MANUAL

Paradise

Sh**!

Snow

Avalanche

sky hook

attack

ROM TRACK side : 2

AUDIO TRACK

1. 1.1.97 / the fall at Shretaad
2. SPIDEAD / KENTARO HAMASATO
3. Sapphire bay - Balinese night flight / MARC NGUYEN TAN
4. whale / Codelaine 804 (www.c404.com)

[CD-ROM TRACK side : 2]
1. 1.1.97 / the fall at Shretaad
2. SPIDEAD / KENTARO HAMASATO
3. Sapphire bay - Balinese night flight / MARC NGUYEN TAN
4. whale / Codelaine 804

PARADISE

How Days of Fun turned into a horrible nightmare

A first hand report from your death-defying employees of abuse industries.

casos REALES!

SENIOR CITIZEN RE-INTEGRATION

ABUSE INDUSTRIES

Shanti Roots
SUBCODEX

Four of these five deejays are absolutely useless.

Da Hool   Hell   Westbam
Spoon   Sven Väth

Your choice.

PUNK ANDERSON

yes, I´ve slept with

linda evangelista
so what´s the big deal?

SUNDAYS 8:00 PM - 2:00 AM

clemens & m-mol, geb.el. gerana. garage. deep & tribal **house**
speedi-o, slack hippy, head etc ambient. dub& space **chillout**

PAVILLON / VOLKSGARTEN

abuse industries: and all your dreams come true

Sons of Ilsa

Shave That Pussy

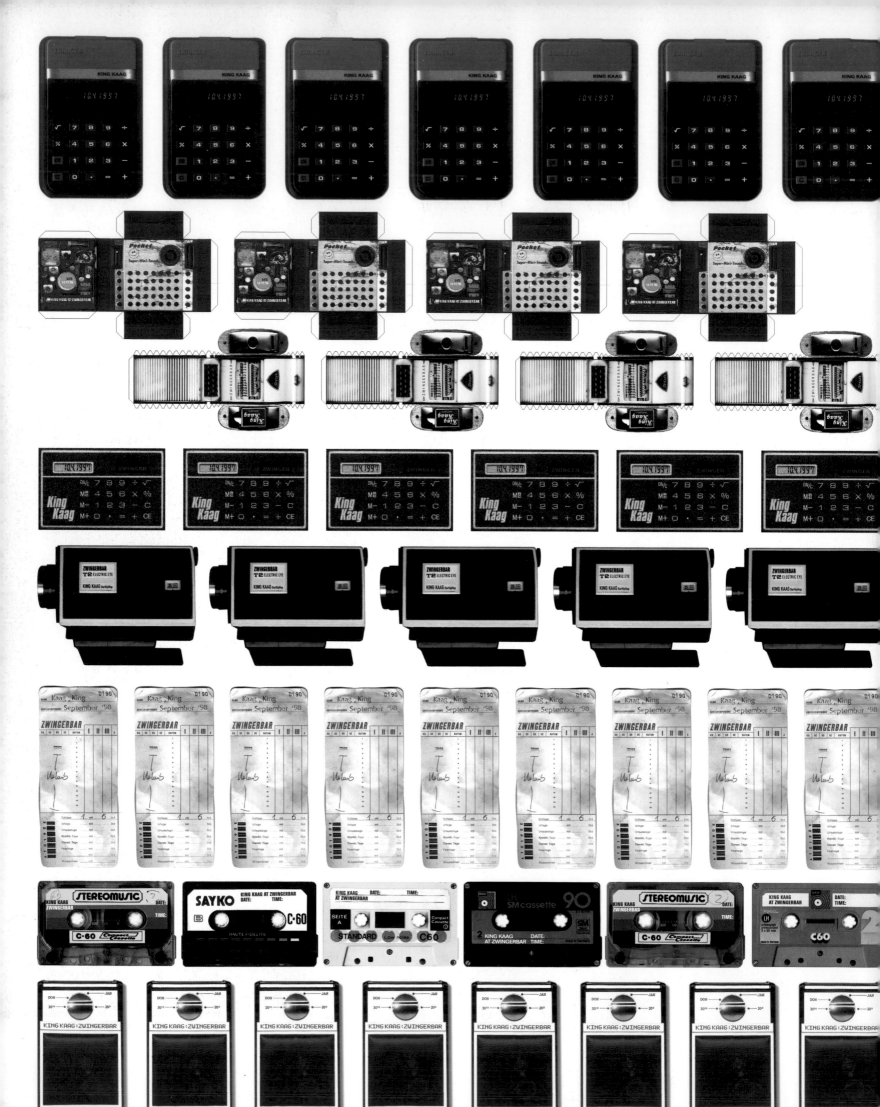

GLAM our

WHERE you sleep

24   25

28

WHO you are

GLAM our

47

44

45   46

43

16

35

46

43

77

TALK IS CHEAP

DESIGN WEAPONN
MAKE
COUNTER
intuition

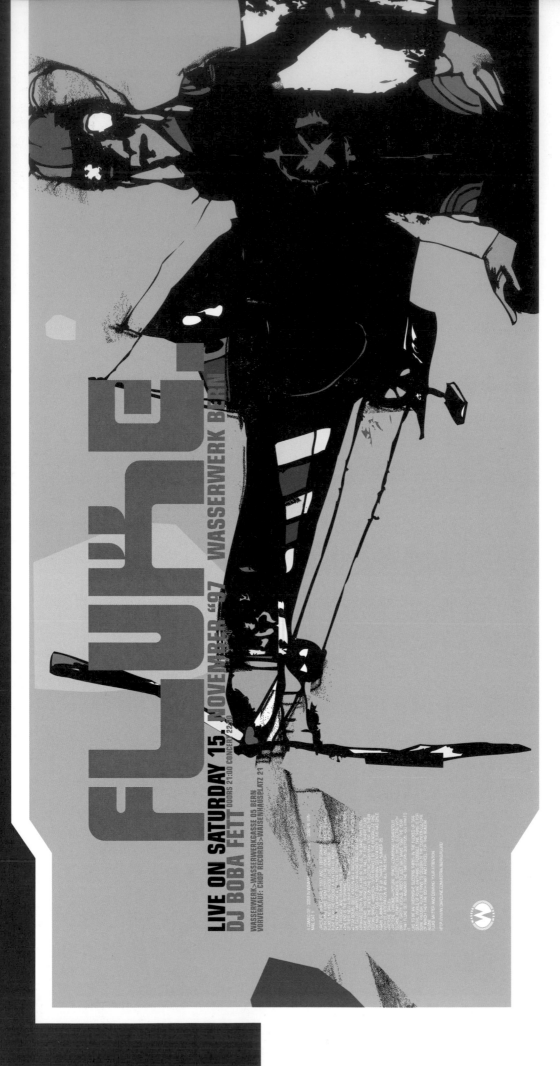

FUTURE

LIVE ON SATURDAY 15 NOVEMBER "97 WASSERWERK BERN
DOORS 21:00 COMEDY 22:00
DJ BOBA FETT

WASSERWERK>WASSERWERKGASSE 05 BERN
VORVERKAUF: CHOP RECORDS>WAISENHAUSPLATZ 21

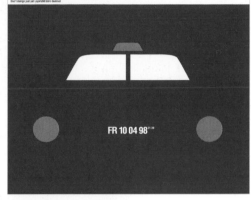

David Holmes Belfast, Northern Ireland
appearing as dj
support dj Curly
Reitschule Bern Dachstock

Vorverkauf: Record Junkie, Krongasse 6, Bern
Don't damage your pet Laptop büro destruct

FR 10 04 98

bürodestruct

mark br**o**om UK

sa.30.05.98 22:00
support DJ's: Ployfex & Federspiel

Dachstock - Reitschule / Bern

Vorverkauf - Record Junkie - Krongasse 6

A/33

B/33

A1. 6 AM PROGRESSIVE MIX
A2. FM INSTRUMENTAL MIX

B1. DISCO INSTRUMENTAL MIX
B2. BREAK YOU DOWN
(FRANKY JONES RMX)

THE
M-EXP
ERIENCE:
THE
TUNNEL

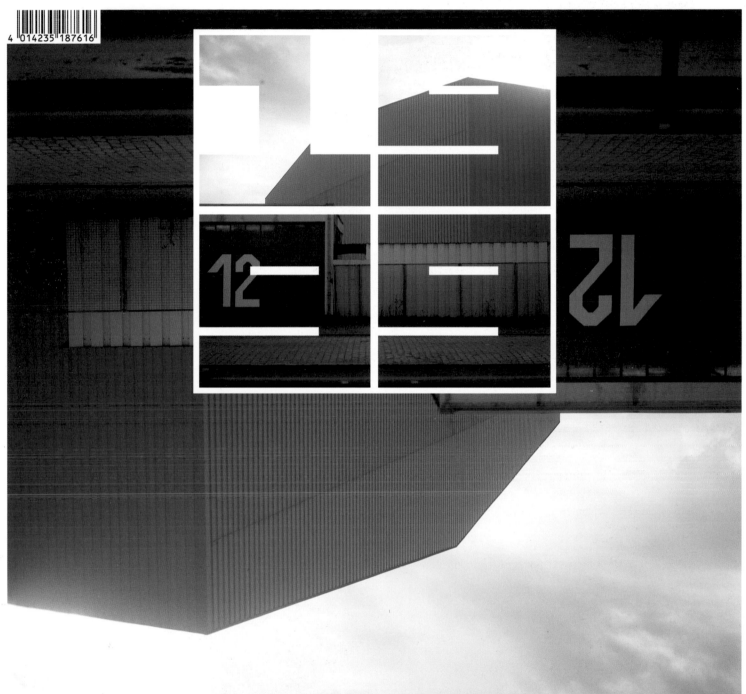

A1: **matt darey remix** 00.09.10 • B1: **original mix** 00.08.33 • AA1: **kay cee remix** 00.06.47 • AA2: **marc et claude's answering machine mix** 00.07.34 • BB1: **paul van dyk remix** 00.09. 49   LC**03193** • DMD**Orbit017**

written and produced by binary finary. published by copyright control. engineered by nuw idol. recorded at the watershed. licensed from aquarius records. track A1remix and additional production by matt darey. track aa1 remix and additional production by kay cee. track aa2 remix and additional production by romboy, derichs and drießen. track bb1 remix and additional production by paul van dyk. cover designed at eikes grafischer hort (www.eikesgrafischerhort.com). (p)1997 aquarius records. (c) 1999 orbit records. orbit records gmbh. lindenallee 58, 20259 hamburg, fax: +49(0)40.432932.32. www.orbit-records.com. made in eu. distributed by discomania.

HELL

MUNICH MACHINE

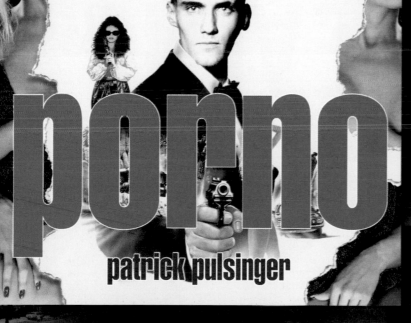

DISKO B & PATRICK PULSINGER PRODUCTIONS PROUDLY PRESENT

porno

patrick pulsinger

22

PISTEPIRKKO
ELEVEN

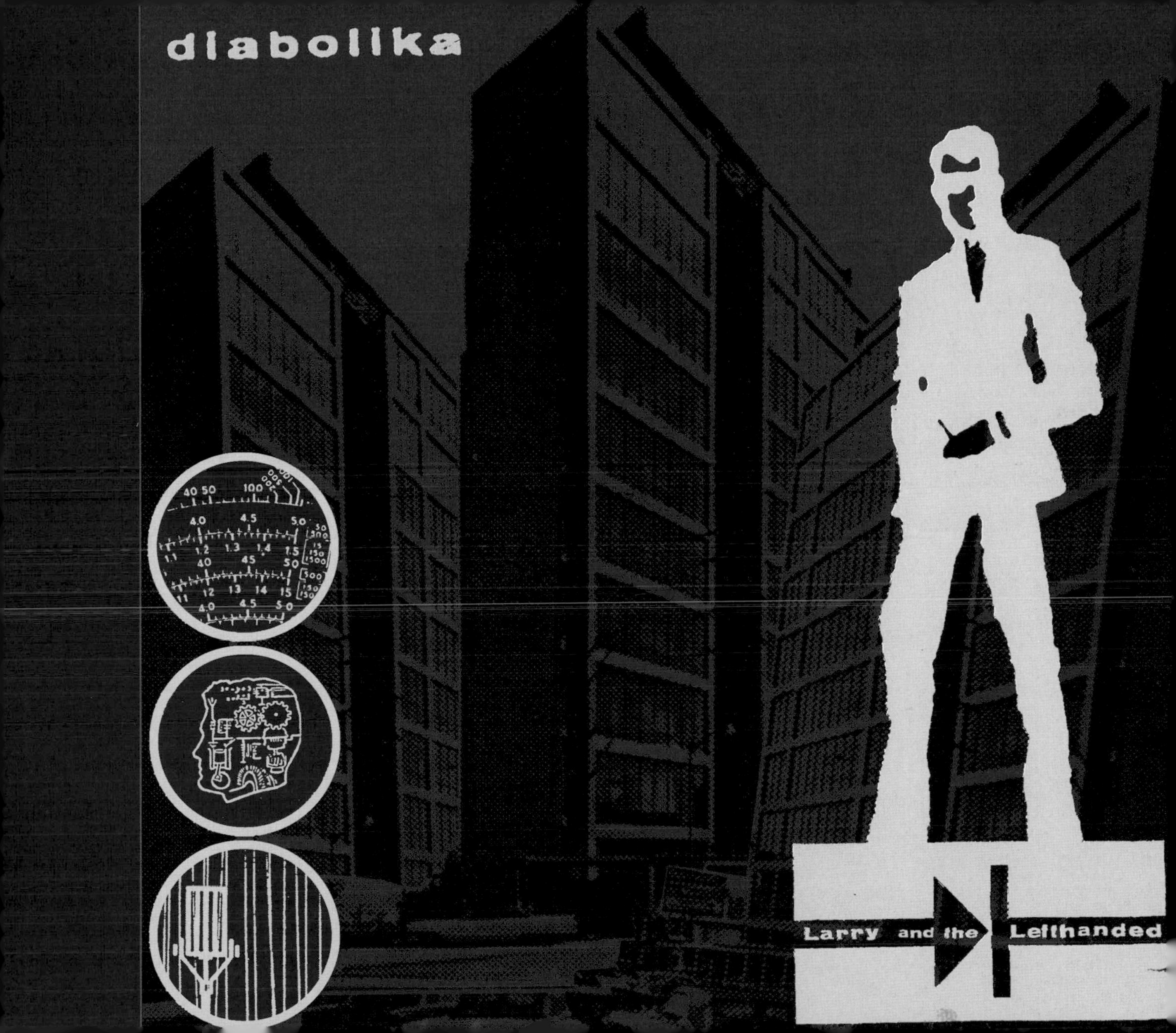
diabolika
Larry and the Lefthanded

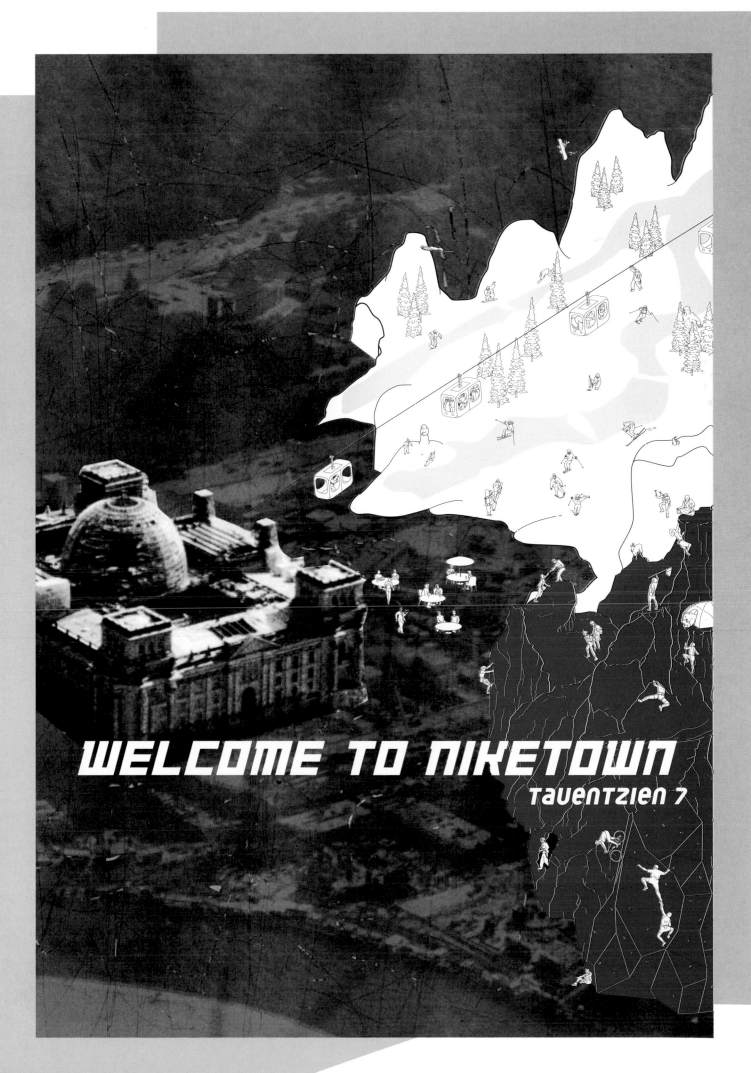

WELCOME TO NIKETOWN

TAUENTZIEN 7

DIESE STRASSE KÖNNTE DIE ERSTE SPIELSTRASSE FÜR BEACH-VOLLEYBALL WERDEN.

ES IST STRENGSTENS VERBOTEN, NICHT AUF DEM RASEN ZU SPIELEN.

WELCOME TO NIKETOWN

NUTZE DEINE STADT AUS.

LASS DICH NICHT VON DEINER STADT AUSNUTZEN.

WELCOME TO NIKETOWN

ES GIBT MEHR SPORTPLÄTZE, ALS DU DENKST. EINER VON IHNEN IST DIREKT UNTER DIESEM POSTER.

WELCOME TO NIKETOWN

HEUTE IST DER RICHTIGE TAG, UM MIT DEM LAUFEN ANZUFANGEN.

WELCOME TO NIKETOWN

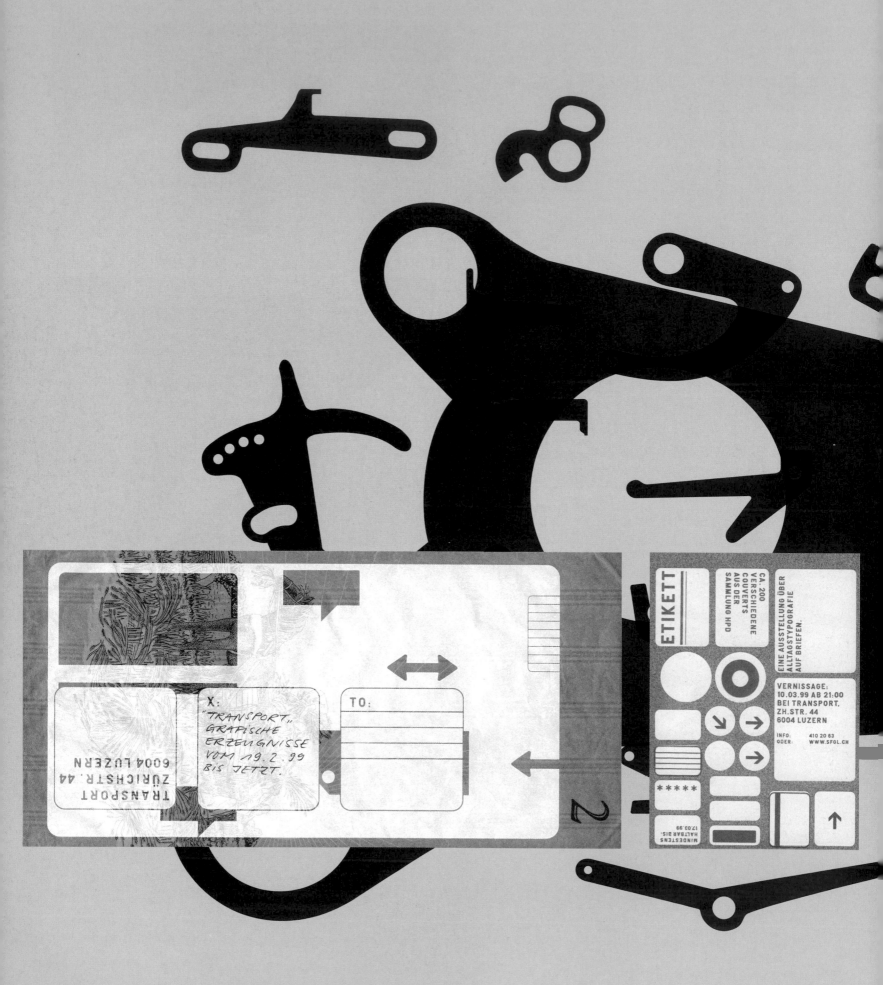

X:
"TRANSPORT,"
GRAFISCHE
ERZEUGNISSE
VOM 19.2.99
BIS JETZT.

TO:

TRANSPORT
ZÜRICHSTR. 44
6004 LUZERN

2

ETIKETT

CA. 200
VERSCHIEDENE
COUVERTS
AUS DER
SAMMLUNG HPD

EINE AUSSTELLUNG ÜBER
ALLTAGSTYPOGRAFIE
AUF BRIEFEN.

VERNISSAGE:
10.03.99 AB 21:00
BEI TRANSPORT,
ZH.STR. 44
6004 LUZERN

INFO: 410 20 63
ODER: WWW.SFGL.CH

MINDESTENS
HALTBAR BIS:
17.03.99

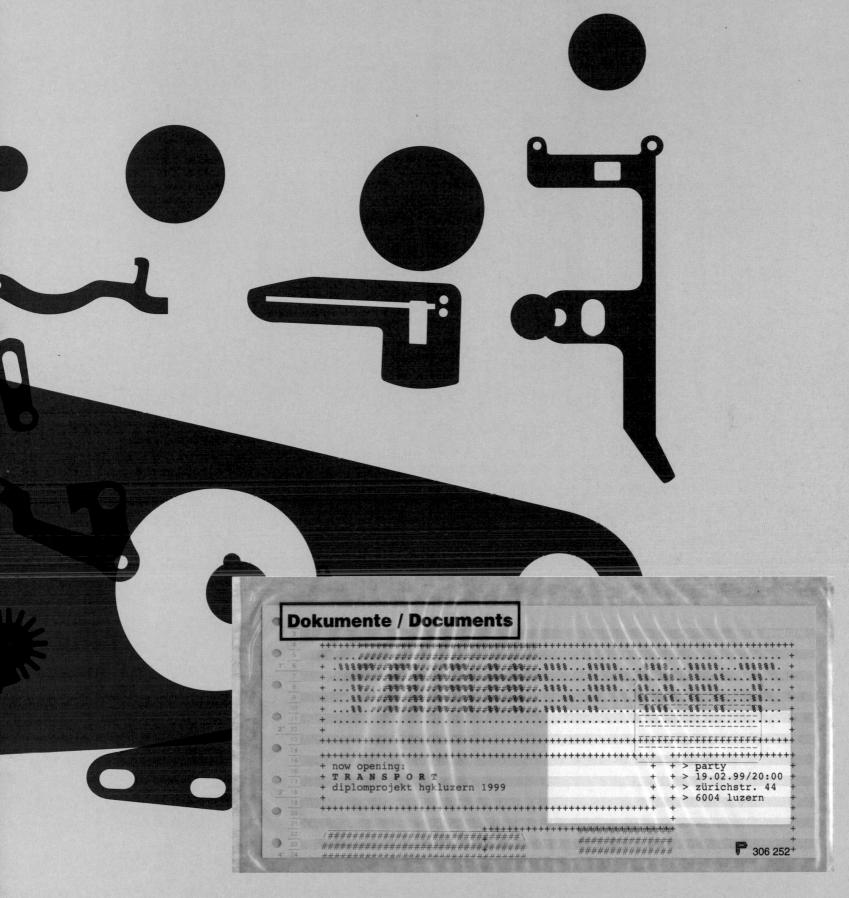

Dokumente / Documents

```
+++++++++++++++++++++++++++++++++++++++++++++++++++++++++++++++++++++++++++++
+ ....#######################################..........................    +
+ ..%%%%%%#%%%%%%%%%%%%%%%%%%%#%%%%...%%%%...%%%%...%%%%...%%%%%...%%%%%%.    +
+ ..%%%%%#%%%%%%%%%%%%%%%%%%%%%#%%%%..%%..%%..%%..%%..%%%%%%%..%%.    +
+ ..%%%%%#%%%%%%%%%%%%%%%%%%%%%#%%%%..%%..%%..%%..%%..%%..%%.    +
+ ..%%..#%%%%%%%%%%%%%%%%%%%%%#%%%%..%%..%%..%%..%%..%%..%%.    +
+ ...................................................................    +
+ .................................................................... +
+++++++++++++++++++++++++++++++++++++++++++++++++++++++++++++++++++++++++++++
+++++++++++++++++++++++++++++++++++++++++++++++++++++++++++++++++++++++++++++
+ now opening:                                    +  + > party           +
+ T R A N S P O R T                               +  + > 19.02.99/20:00   +
+ diplomprojekt hgkluzern 1999                    +  + > zürichstr. 44    +
+                                                 +  + > 6004 luzern      +
+++++++++++++++++++++++++++++++++++++++++++++++++++++++++++++++++++++++++++++
/####################################                ##############
#######################################              ##############
##########################################           ##############
```

306 252⁺

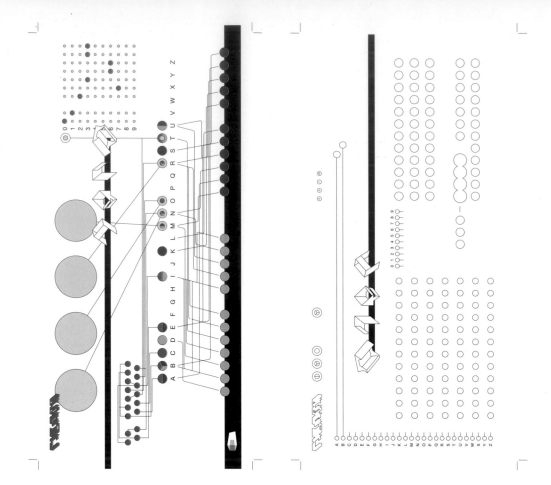

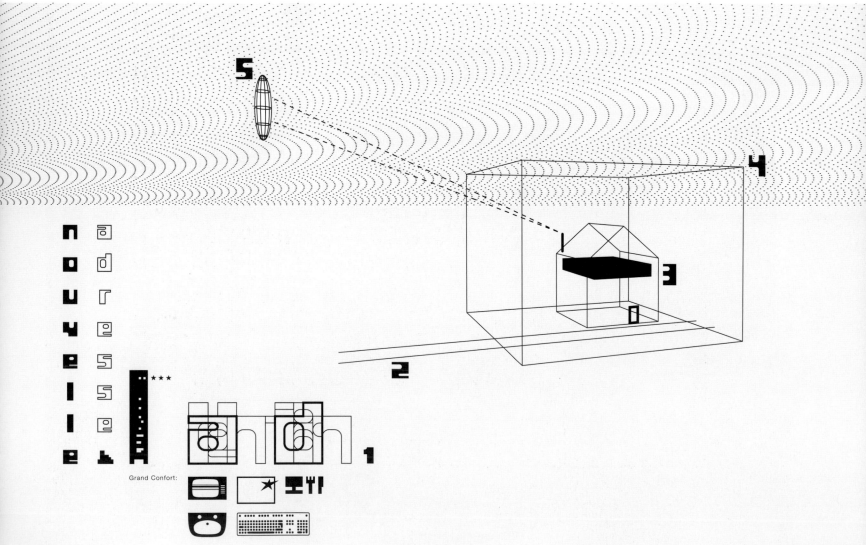

Grand Confort:

nouvelle

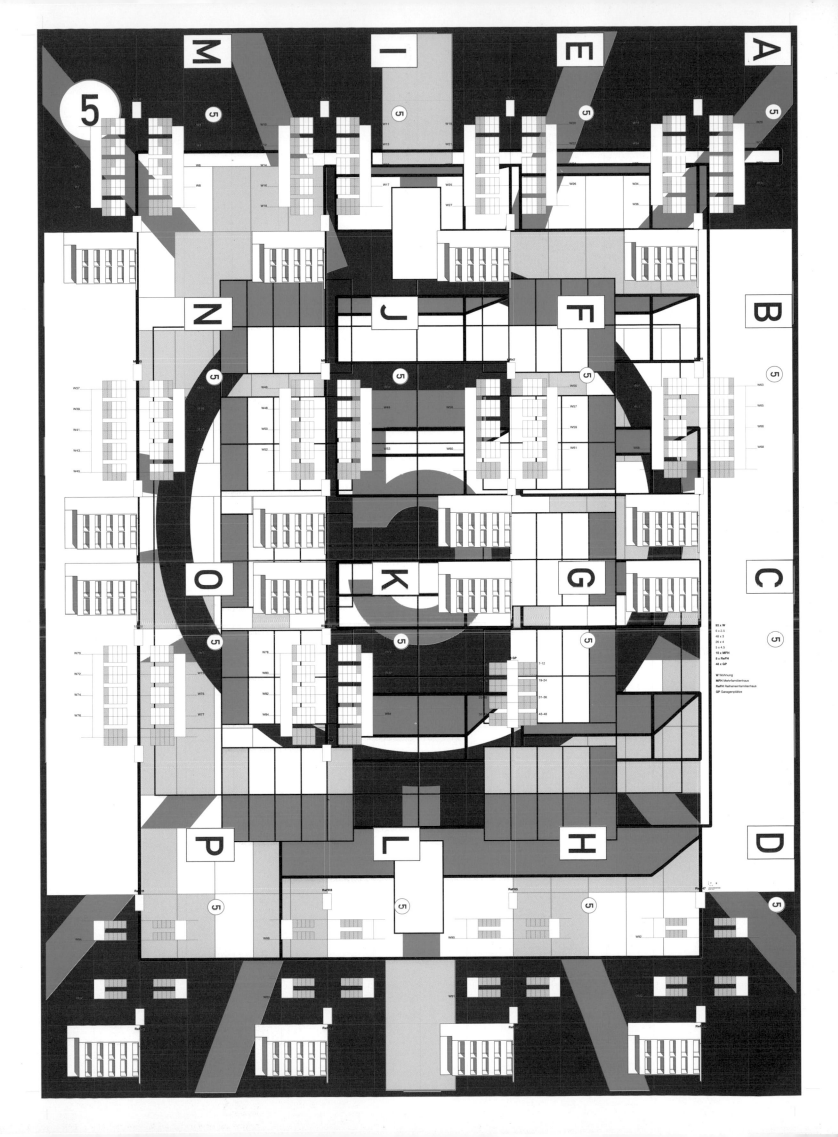

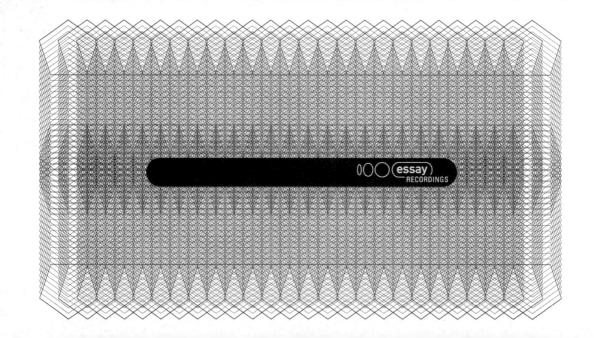

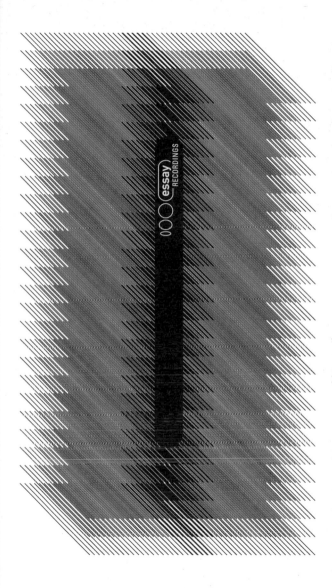

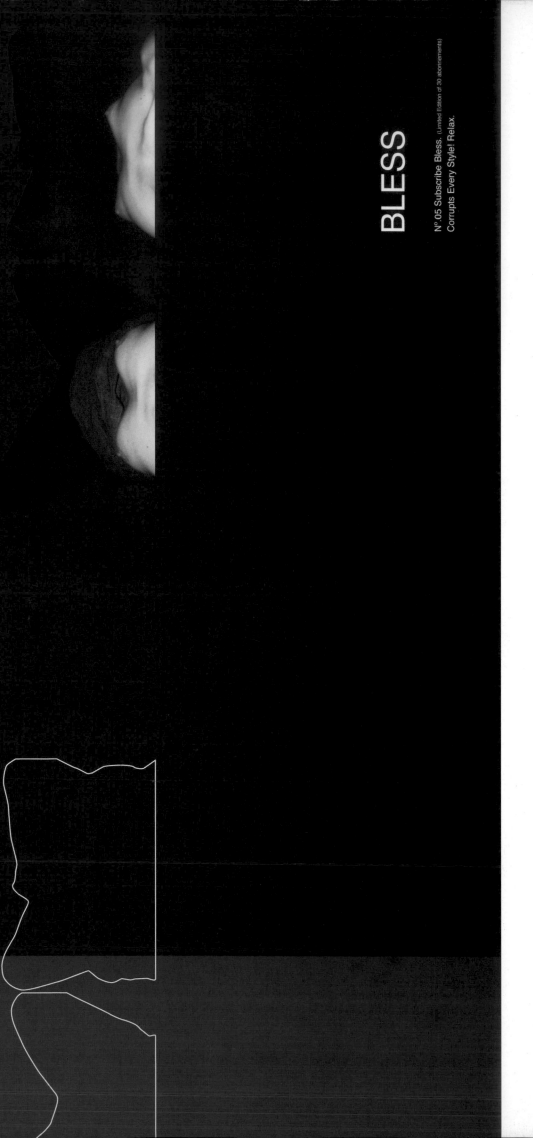

BLESS

Nº 05 Subscribe Bless. (Limited Edition of 30 abonnements)
Corrupts Every Style! Relax.

serving suggestion:

www.stylorouge.co.uk www.24seven.co.uk www.richardjames.co.uk
www.richardjames.co.uk www.stricklandfairhurst.co.uk www.24seven.co.uk
www.stricklandfairhurst.co.uk www.trilokgurtu.co.uk www.stylorouge.co.uk
www.trilokgurtu.co.uk www.stylorouge.co.uk www.richardjames.co.uk
www.stylorouge.co.uk www.24seven.co.uk www.richardjames.co.uk
www.richardjames.co.uk www.stricklandfairhurst.co.uk

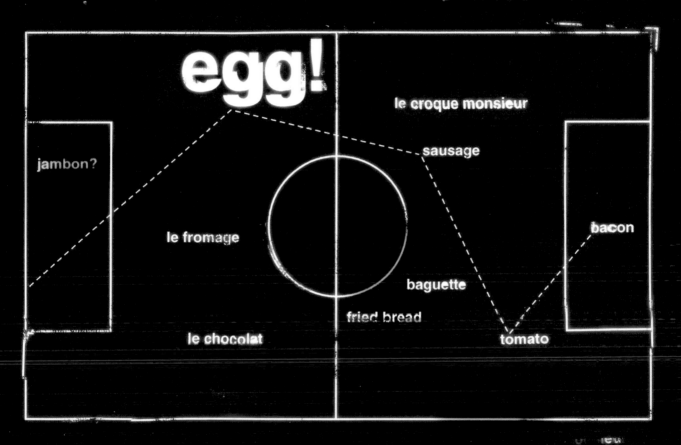

egg!

le croque monsieur

sausage

jambon?

bacon

le fromage

baguette

fried bread

le chocolat

tomato

A full report will follow here shortly...

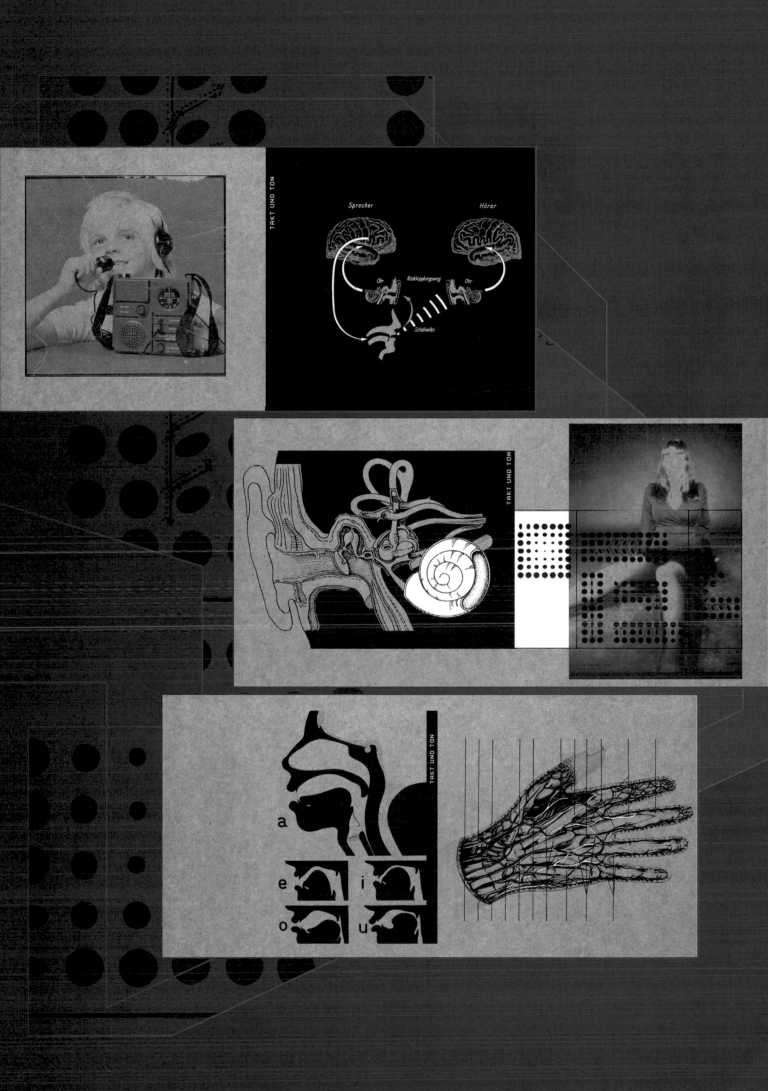

TAKT UND TON

Sprecher   Hörer

Ohr   Rückkopplungsweg   Ohr

Schallwellen

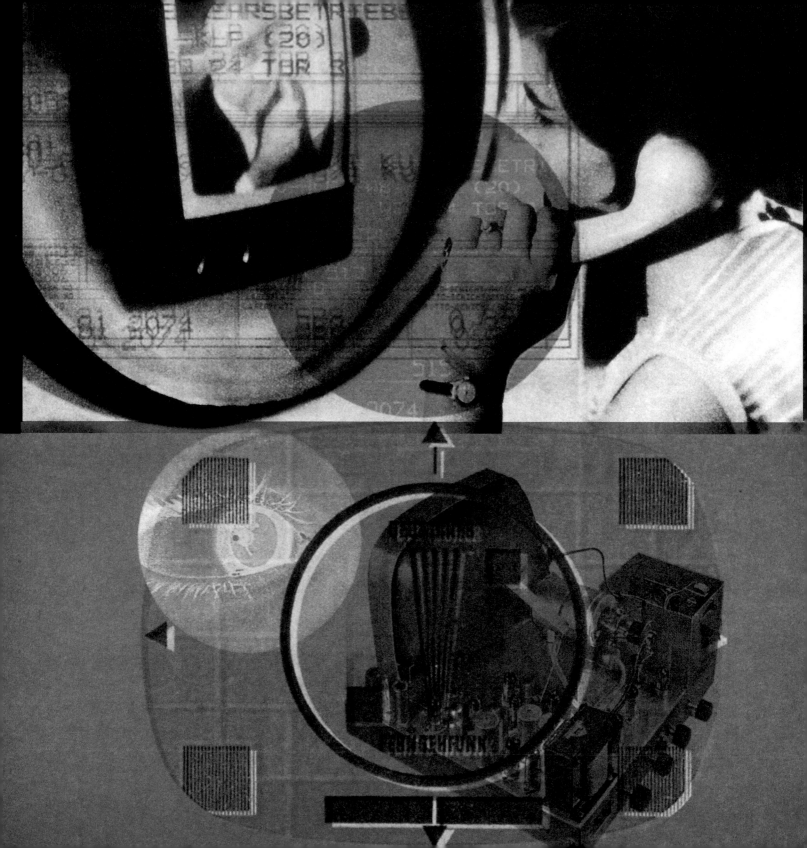

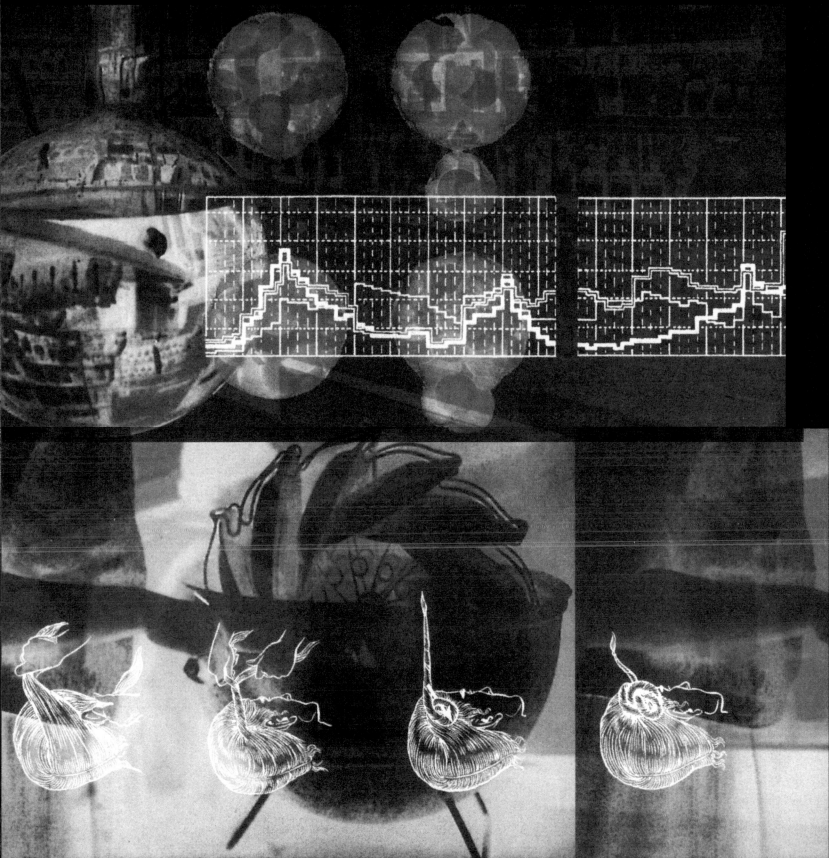

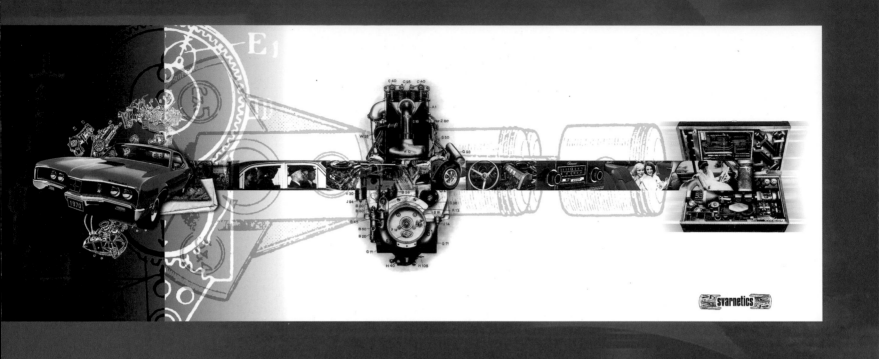

svarnetics

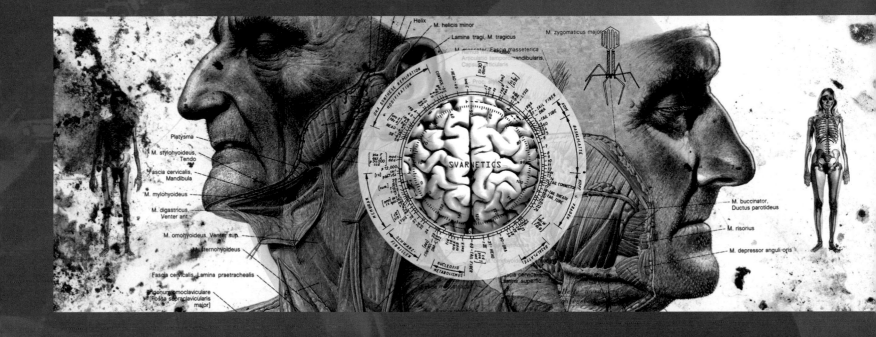

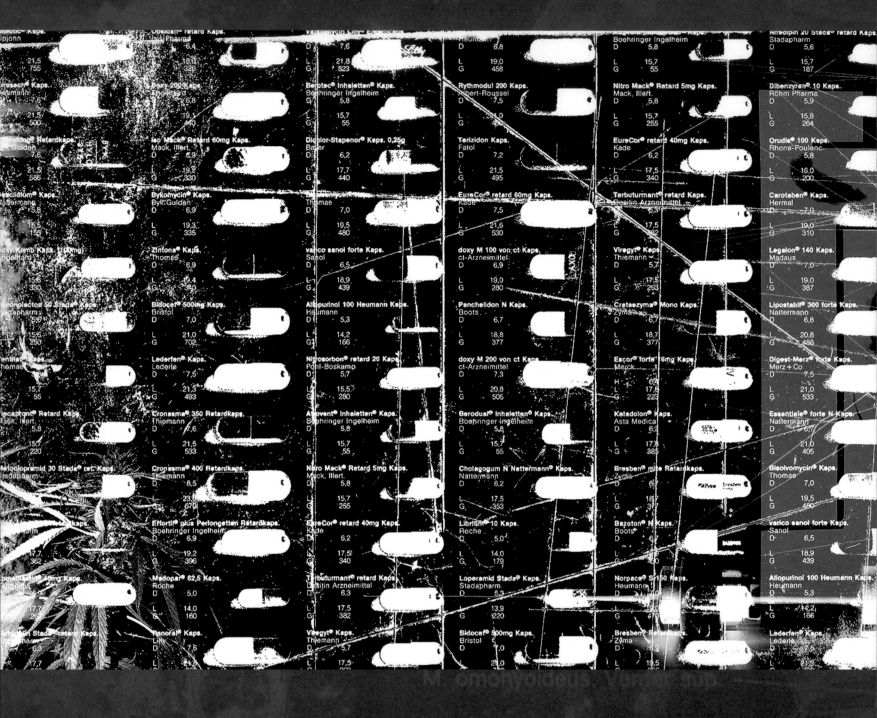

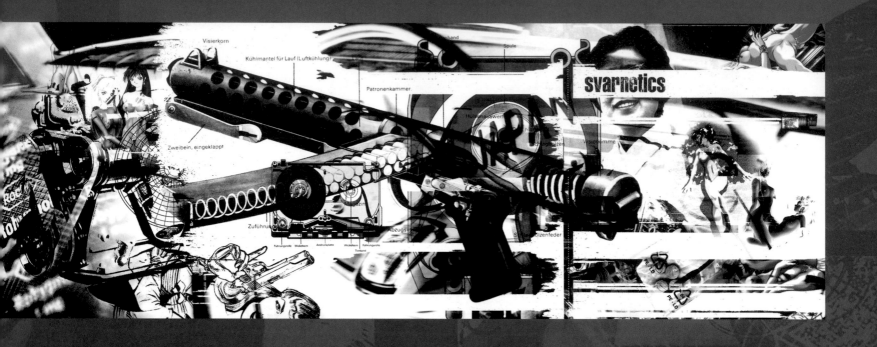

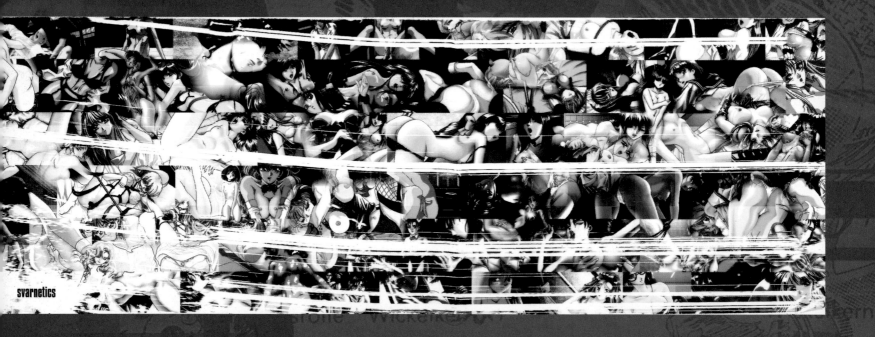

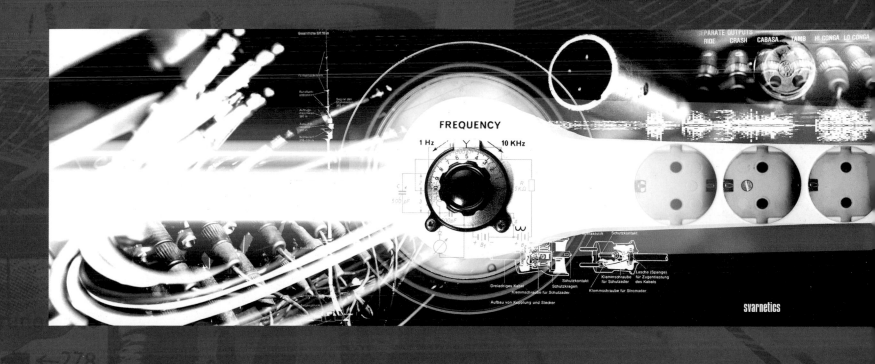

svarnetics

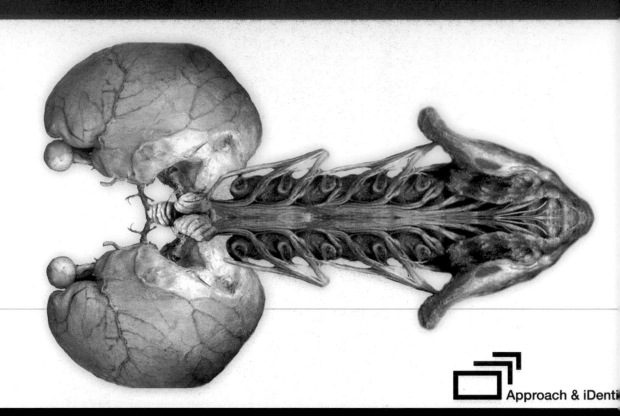

Approach & iDenti[fy]

Approach & iDentify

38-357
RN
BB
158 Gr

A

DIRECT

DISECT

jörg burkhardt

der rückgekoppelte satz

wollte sage sasasagengen

ich gehe jetzt nana wollte sa wo i

sasasagengen
jewoosajewoll
seine hellen u
will/kannatürli
sind voll als ic
schwüle eines
durchräuchen
sagen ich geh
auf provisierte
texten jedes d
aus digitalen t
auslesen wie
schraube ...

engpol
medien
social beat kalender 95

Schwüle in der Nacht.
Irgendwo das Grollen eines Gewitters.
Eingetrocknete Essensreste
auf den Tellern.
Reggae.
Manchmal wehten die Topfpflanzen
am geöffneten Fenster im Wind.
Es sah aus, als lachten sie.
Sandra stellte
eine Obstplatte auf den Tisch.
Carlo legte ein Stück Shit daneben.
Zum Geburtstag, sagte er.
Damit wirst du Sandra
keine Freude machen,
sagte Thomas.
Sie verträgt es nicht mehr.
Der Kreislauf.
Aber dir macht er eine Freude damit,
sagte Sandra.
Und wenn du glücklich bist,
dann bin ich es auch.
Sie lachten.
Waren vollgefressen.
Aber angenehm.
Ein Gefühl wie Italien.
An der Heizung trocknete Wäsche.
Da kannte Sandra kein Erbarmen.
Auch im August nicht.
Die Heizung läuft ja nur auf Stufe zwei,

Seperator

'ZIGNS_BOUQUET/DEMO ¬¬#1_JAMES
(PERFECT_INSTINCT)5:04_#2_BARK
UP_THE_WRONG_TREE_3:58_#3_MOON
PLACES_5:08¬¬ALL_SONGS_BY_'ZI
NES_BOUQUET¬¬REC._FROM_APRIL
27TH_TO_29TH¬¬REC./MIXED/MAST
ERED_@_MRS_RECORDS/NIEDERWANGE
N¬¬PRODUCED_BY_'ZINES_BOUQUET
MUSICANS:_SULU»VOCALS/ROGER_RU
TSCHI»GUITARS/ANDREJ_PANIC»DRU
MS/IVO_UBEZIO»BASS¬¬GUESTS:_
BEN_VATTER»TRUMPET_ON_"JAMES"/
TOBIAS_GURTNER»HAMMOND_ON_"MOO
N_PLACES"¬¬des._marc_kappeler
CONTACT:_T/F_++41_31_312_43_25

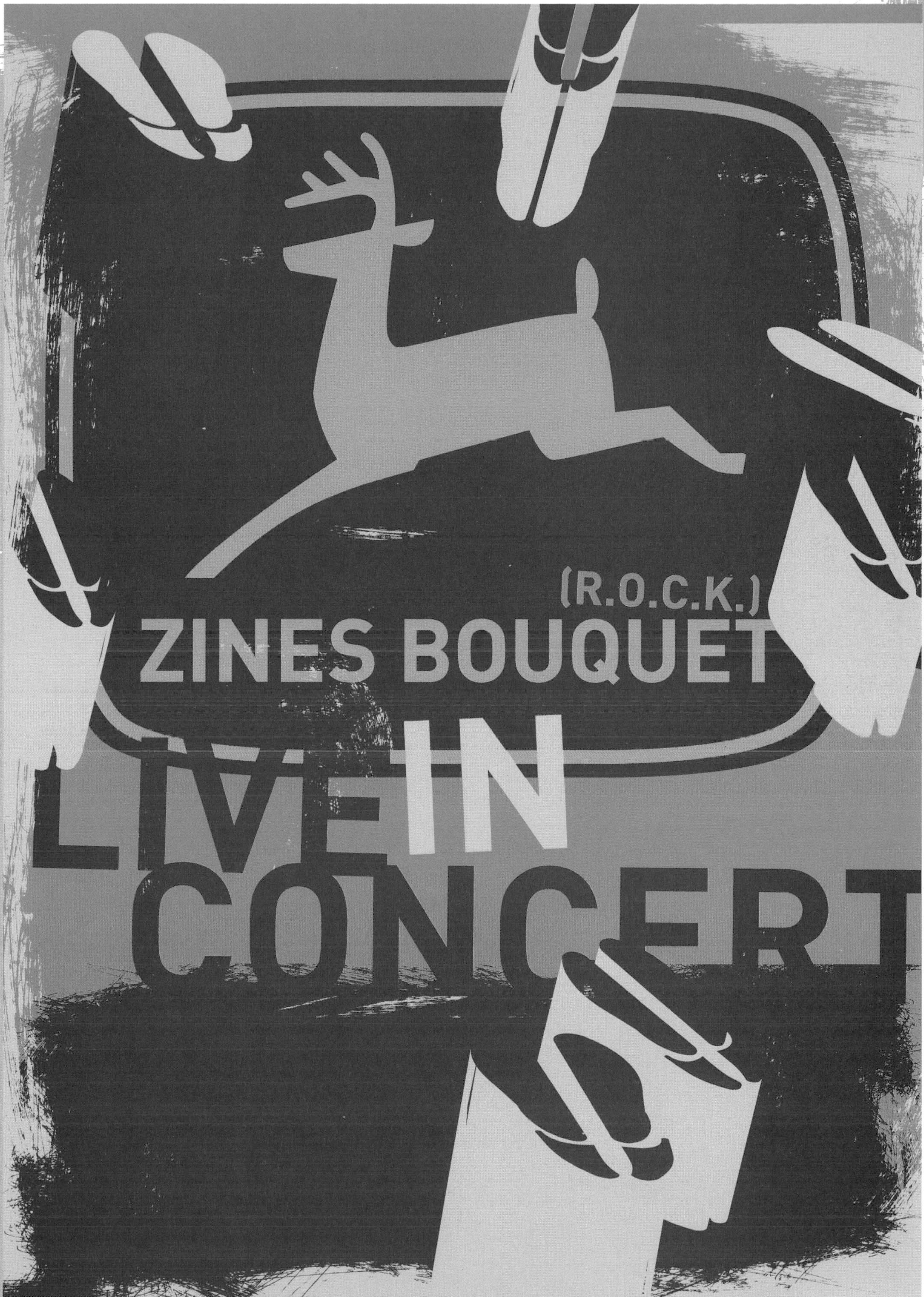
(R.O.C.K.)
ZINES BOUQUET
LIVE IN
CONCERT

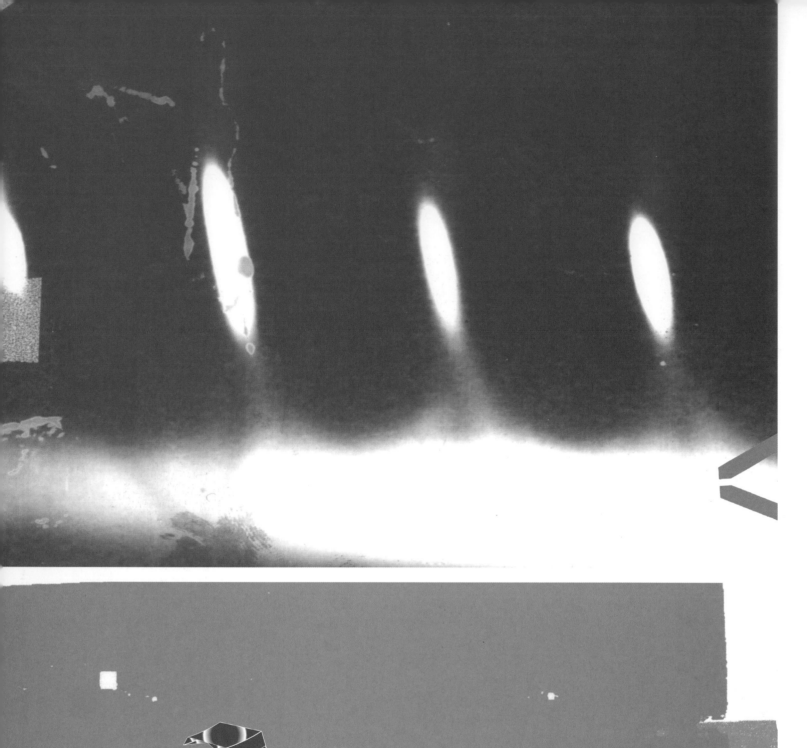

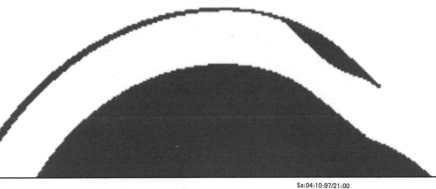

Sa:04:10:97/21:00
Poets of Rhythm (D)
Der wahrscheinlich beste Funk-Act aus deutschen Landen.
Very seventies,
very rude,
very funky
- get it down,
Goddam'.

Fr:03:10:97/21:00
Srictly Massive
DJs: M.F. (United Tribes Records)/Sensi (UTR Empire, Drum FM)/Lockee (UTR Empire, Drum FM)
/Switch (Resident Strictly Massive). MCs: Shoka (UTR Empire)/Fight (UTR Empire)
Mit Strictly Massive startet der Gaskesel eine Serie von Drum'n'Bass Events, die einerseits lokalen
und internationalen Heroes, aber auch Newcomern eine Plattform bieten soll.

Fr:10:10:97/21:00
Pool: Phresh and Pharty
DJs Dan Curtin (USA)/V-KEY (Berne)/Chill-In by Marco Repeto
Dan Curtin aus Cleveland (USA) ist einer der gefragtesten DJs und Produzenten der Welt.
Davon zeugen seine zahlreichen DJ-Auftritte rund um den Globus und seine unzähligen
Plattenveröffetlichungen auf Labels wie Peacefrog UK, Sublime Japan, Strictly Rhythm
USA oder seinem eigenen Imprint Metamorphic

Sa:11:10:97/21:00
World of House
Paradise Production presents: Ibiza Night

House Floor:
DJ Nicky Holloway (Cream, Amnesia)
DJ Alfredo (KU, Pacha, Space)
DJ Johnny Walker (Cream, Amnesia)
Dj Luca (Resident Jockey Club)

Progressive Floor:
Franctone (U1)
DJ Dainskin (Take 5)
DJ Christopher S. (Nachtwerk)

Chill Out/Ambiente Floor:
DJ Roberto Mas
The Conga Machine

Decoration by Penelope, Paris

OpenEndParty!

Fr:17:10:97/21:00
Frauendisco Welle

Fr:24:10:97/21:00
Groove Attack
Pearls of Jazz, Acid Jazz, Funk and Latin
DJ Stomp and DJ Spark

●● oktoberfest

gaskessel, Sandrainstrasse 25, 3007 Bern
InfoLine: 031/372 40 00

Fr:31:10:97/21:00
KO1: Classic Chessu Sound mit DJ Tarcis

Fr:31:10:97/21:00
KO2: Live in Concert: Fast Lane

YOUNG NECROMUHI

PFADFIN
DEREI.MITTE

BERLINRAUSCH FUER INTERKONTINENTALE LIEBESTAETER

 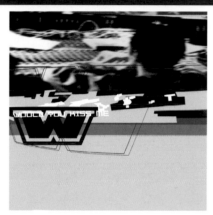 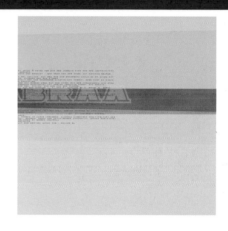 

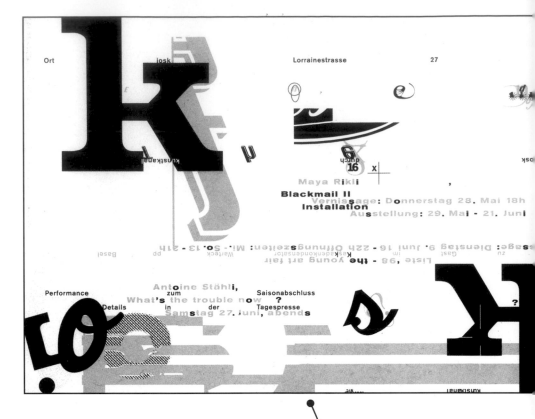

Ort   iosk   Lorrainestrasse   27

Maya Rikli   ,
Blackmail II
Vernissage: Donnerstag 28. Mai 18h
Installation
                    Ausstellung: 29. Mai - 21. Juni

Dienstag 9. Juni 16 - 22h Öffnungszeiten: Mi.- So. 13 - 21h

Liste '98 - the young art fair

Performance   Antoine Stähli,   Saisonabschluss
            zum   ?
What's the trouble now   ?
Details   in   der   Tagespresse
            Samstag 27. Juni, abends   ?

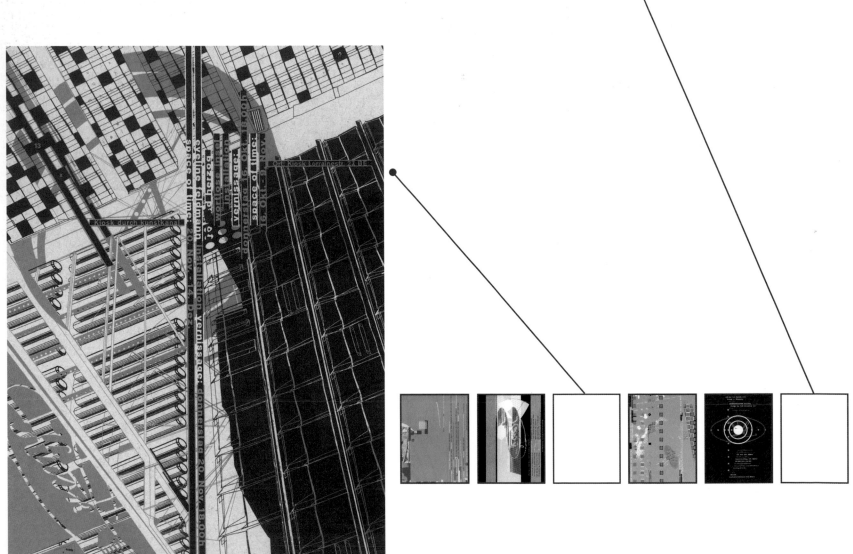

FR.31.JULY*

JET*STREAM*

:INSEL:ALT.TREPTOW.6

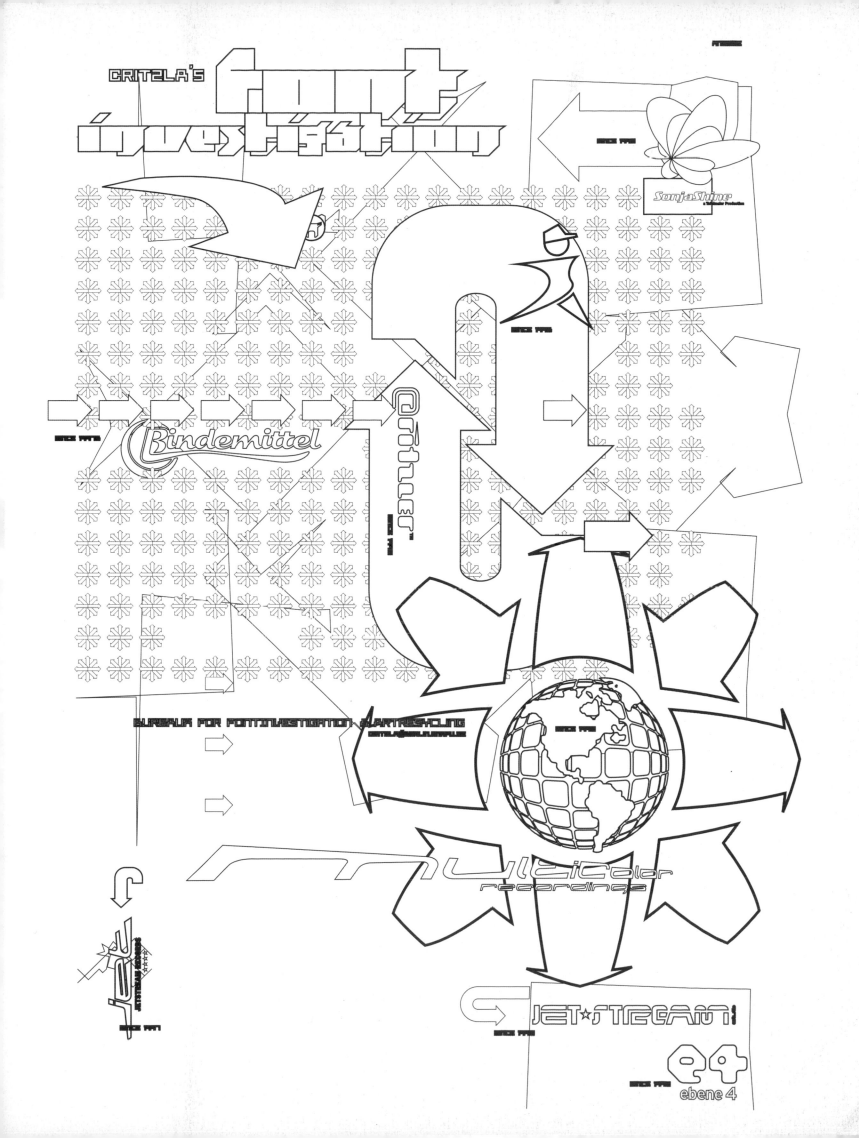

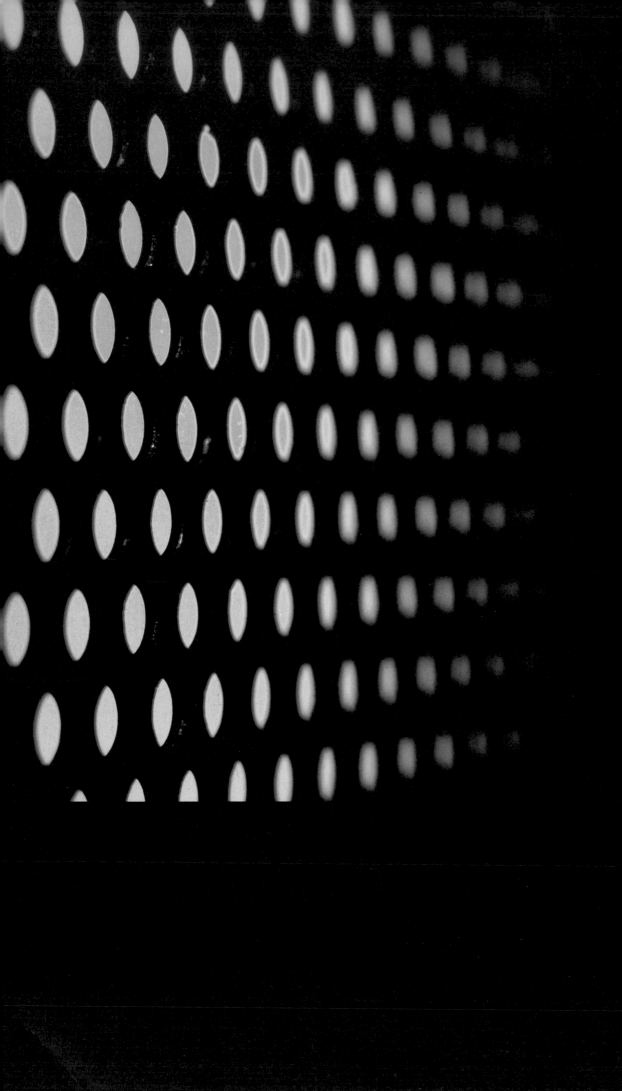

hydra:sonic:fiction>landscapes
Y
H
D
R
A
> location:unidentified
> re:enter code

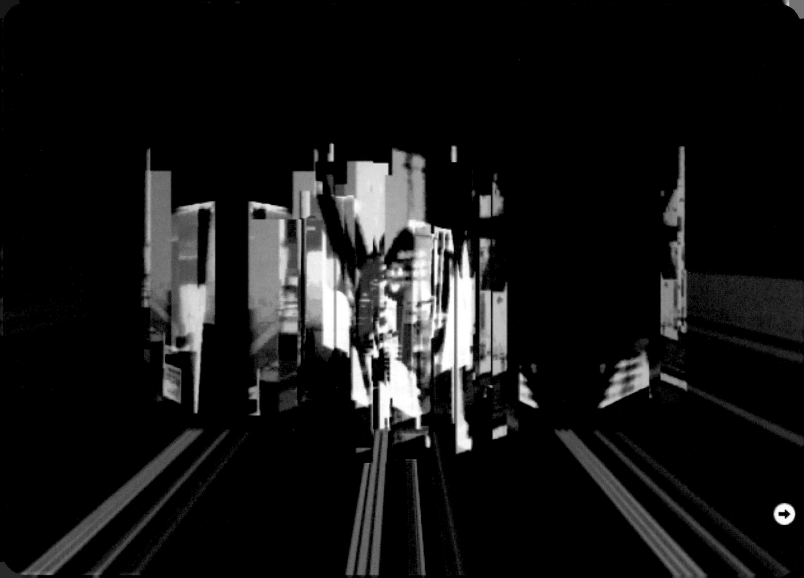

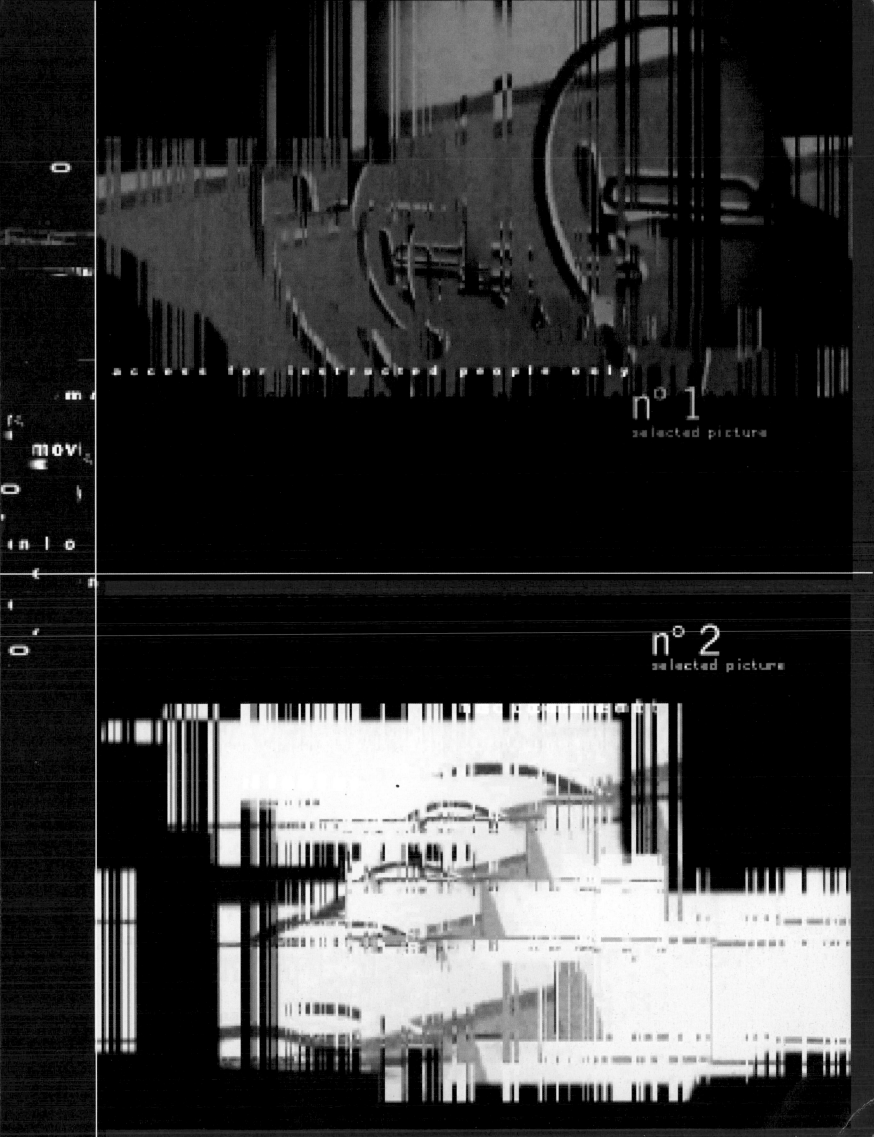

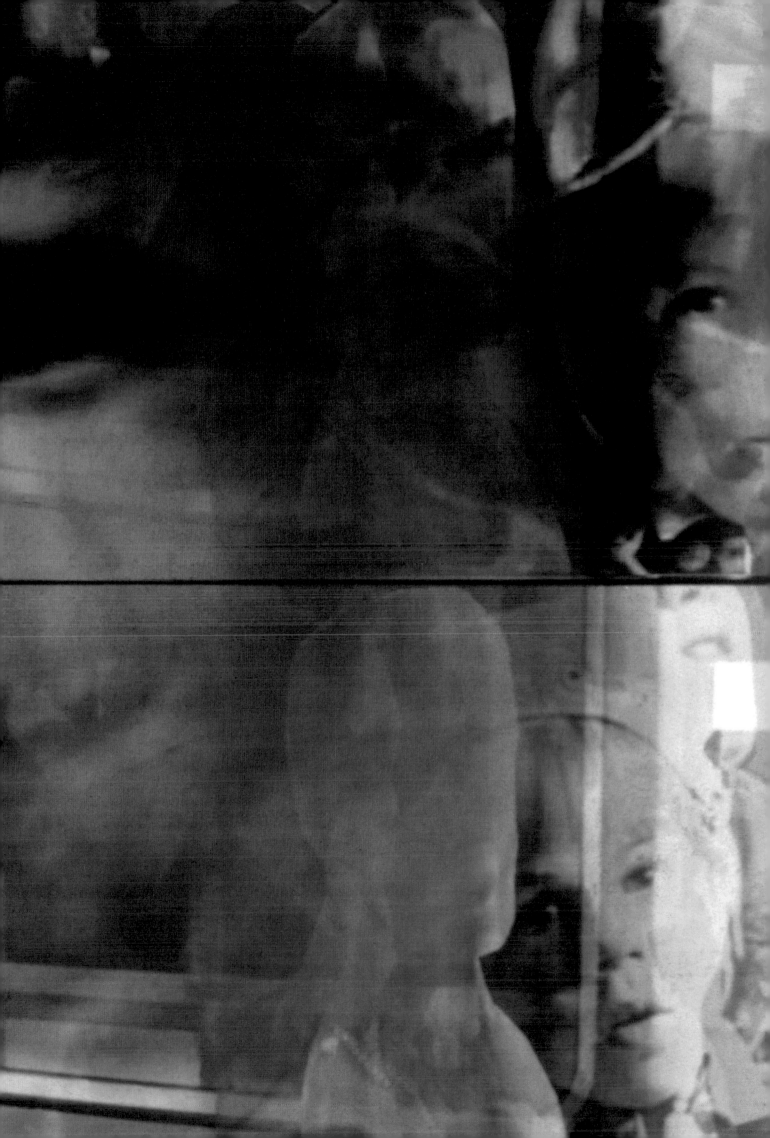

SELECT

NEXT
CLIP

00:37

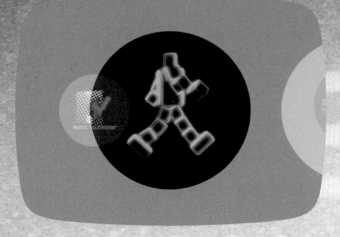
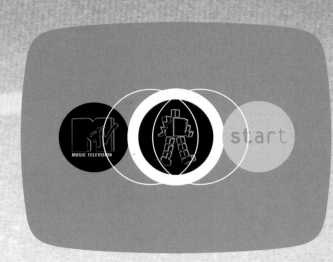
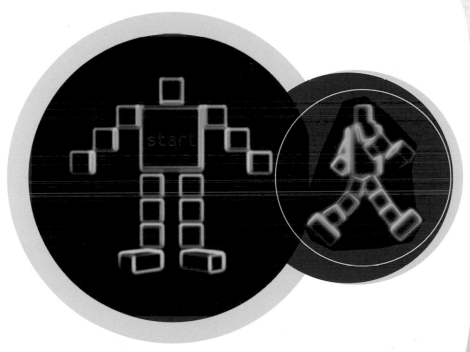

Jam & Spoon
STELLA 1999 - 1992
How Stella Got Her Groove Back

*West*bam **2**

Tall Paul

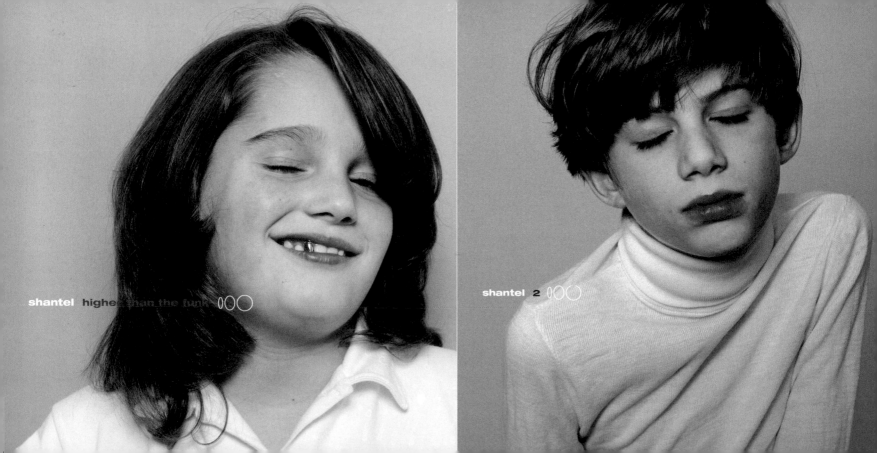

shantel highee than the funk)()()

shantel 2)()()

shantel | oh so lovely

shantel ep ◎○○

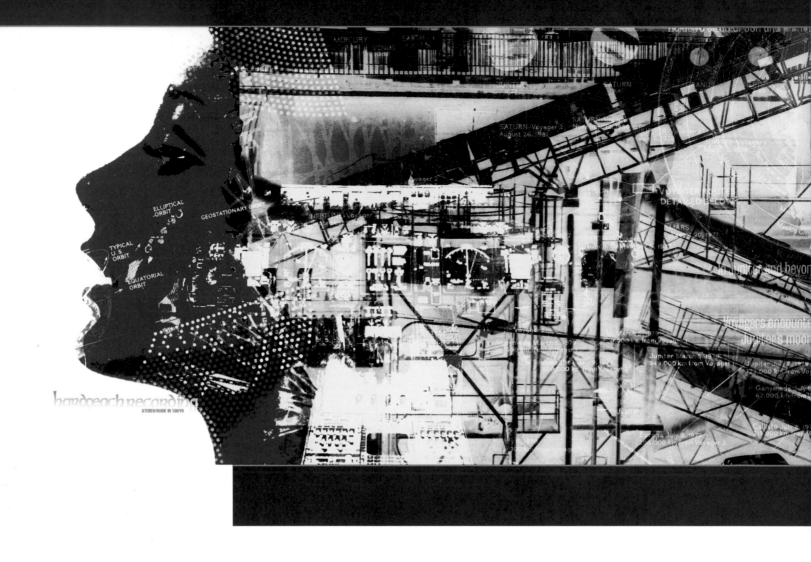

KING CAY LAB. / RM° 1003 15-1 NANPEIDAI-CHO, SHIBUYA-KU, TOKYO PHONE : 81 3 54 56 40 44 FAX : 81 3 37 70 93 34
TOSHIAKI UCHIKOSHI / RYO ASADA / SHINNOICHI YOSHIDA / MAIKO YOSHINO / YASUSHI YAMAGUCHI

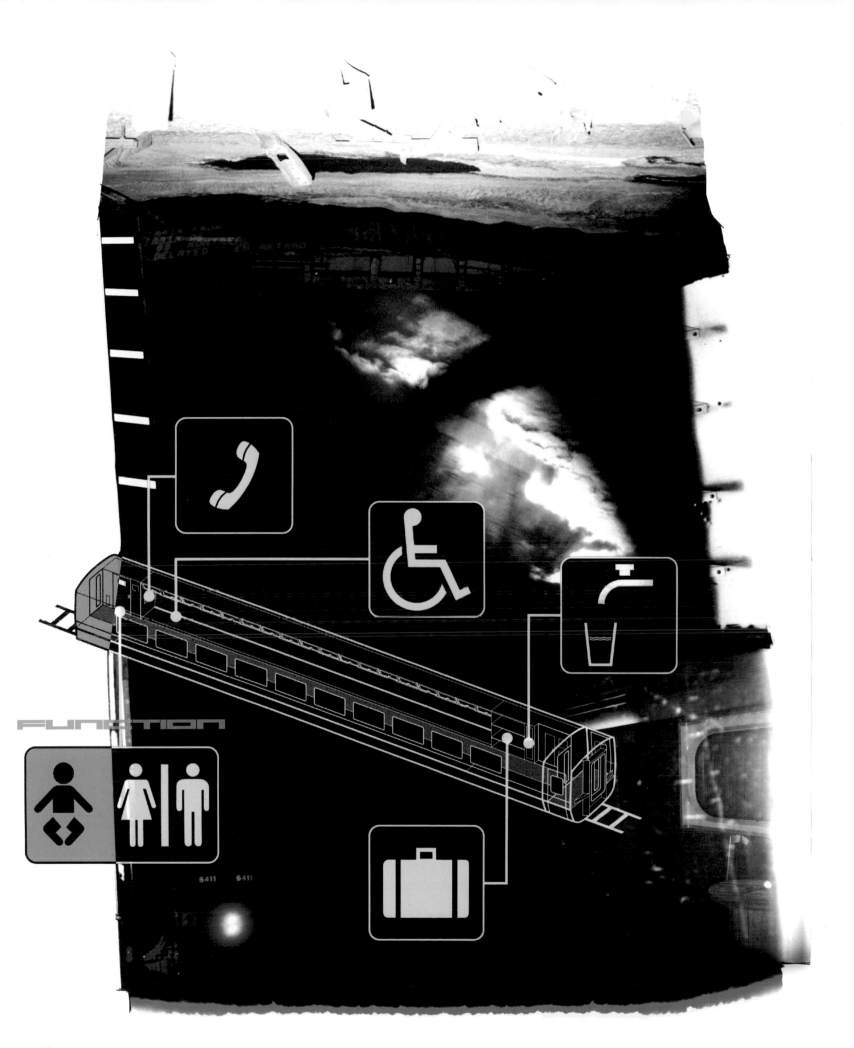

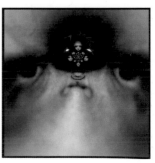

KREISEL 99/1

STUDIO672

de homici diary

ISBN 0-8149106-1 0

all tracks written and produced by jammie neil &

KREISEL 99/2

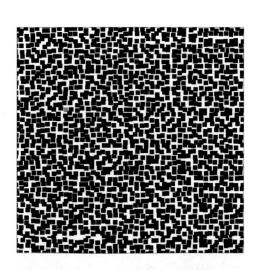

STUDIO 672

SWISSAIR **boy** / *smart* products

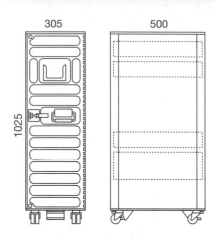

305   500

1025

No.
Nummerierte, limitierte Auflage

Original Swissair Boy gebraucht, rot, Preis 484.-- inkl. 4 Schubladen
andere Farben ab 3 Stk. Aufpreis 101.--/Stk.

470

80   Kleine Schublade 20.--

140   Grosse Schublade 30.--

smart products© ist nicht Mehrwertsteuerpflichtig

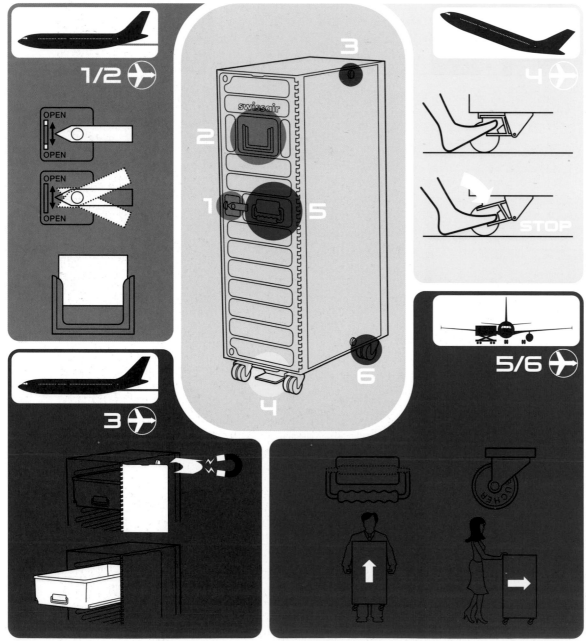

1/2 ✈

OPEN
OPEN

OPEN
OPEN

3

2

1   5

4 ✈
STOP

3 ✈

5/6 ✈

4

6

France 98
38 STADE DE JOSEF

France 98
B
38 STADE DE JOSEF

France 98
38 STADE DE JOSEF

France 98
38 STADE DE JOSEF

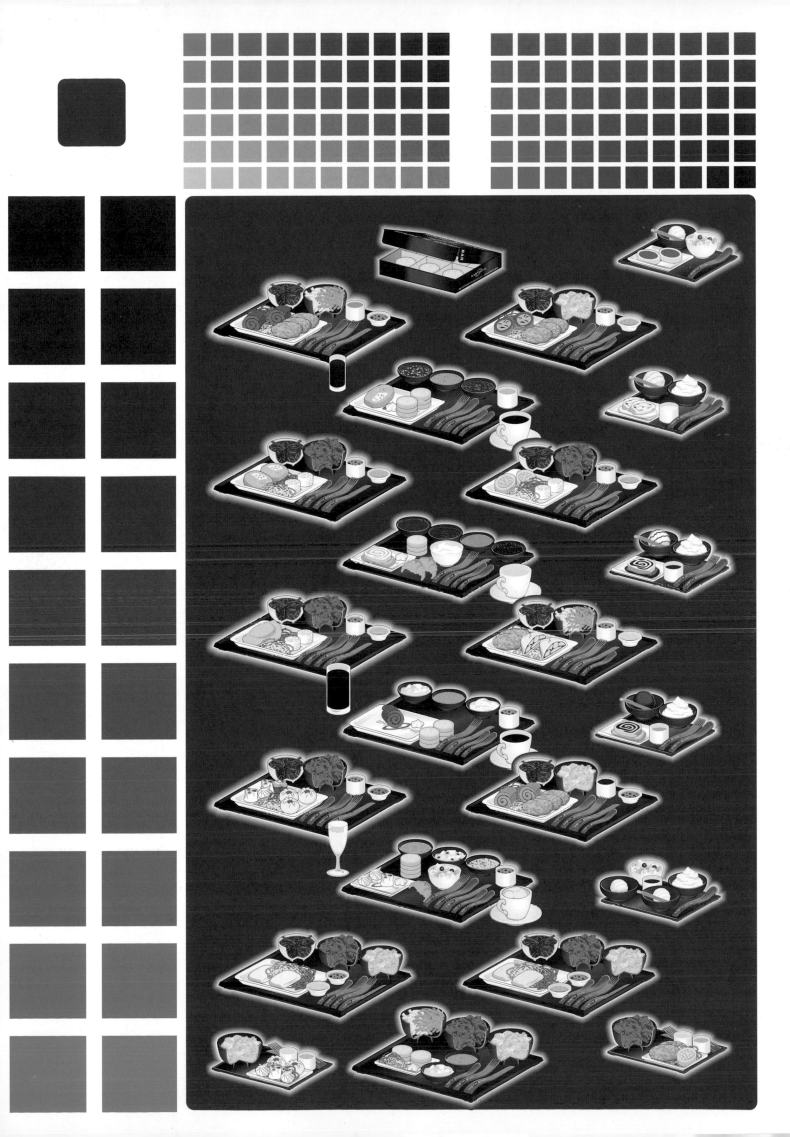

RETTET
DIE MENSCHHEIT
AUS DER SEENOT DER REALITÄT

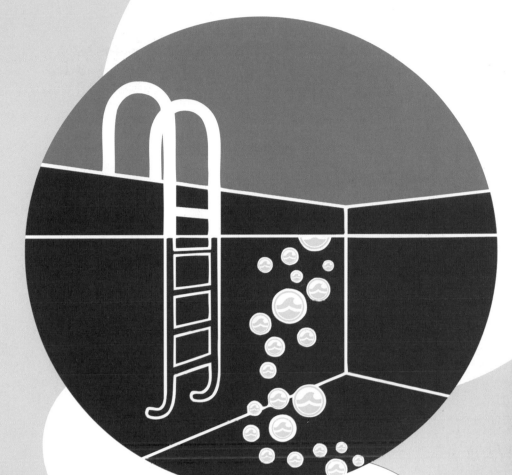

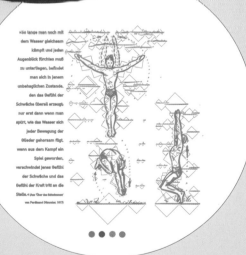

»So lange man noch mit
dem Wasser gleichsam
kämpft und jeden
Augenblick fürchten muß
zu unterliegen, befindet
man sich in jenem
unbehaglichen Zustande,
den das Gefühl der
Schwäche überall erzeugt,
nur erst dann wenn man
spürt, wie das Wasser sich
jeder Bewegung der
Glieder gehorsam fügt,
wenn aus dem Kampf ein
Spiel geworden,
verschwindet jenes Gefühl
der Schwäche und das
Gefühl der Kraft tritt an die
Stelle.« (Aus "Über das Schwimmen"
von Ferdinand Dilmanns, 1817)

● ● ● ●

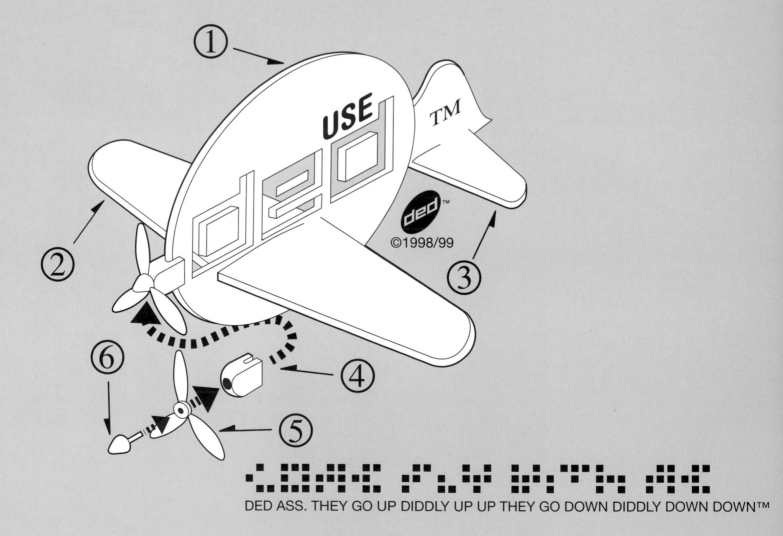

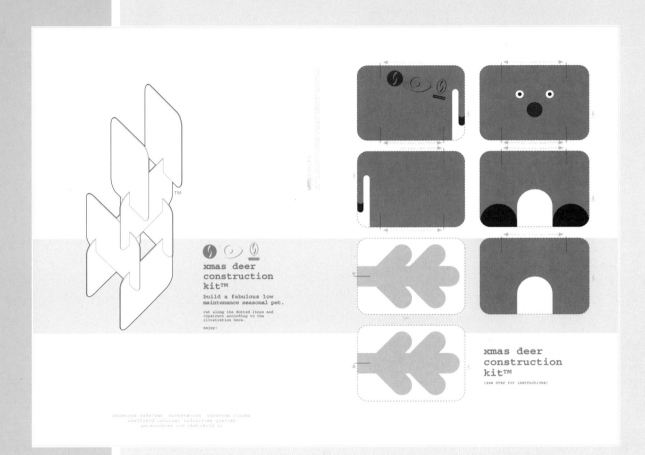

**xmas deer
construction
kit™**

build a fabulous low
maintenance seasonal pet.

cut along the dotted lines and
construct according to the
illustration here.

enjoy!

**xmas deer
construction
kit™**

(see over for instructions)

showroom cafe/bar workstation showroom cinema
sheffield cultural industries quarter
paternoster row sheffield s1

盗難防止

reject. v0.1

Esso vuole rappresentare, ospitando pagine da
chiunque le voglia fornire o mediante link ad altri
siti, tutto il panorama speleo nazionale.

pagine da chiunque

partecipazione di chiunque sia interessato alla
speleologia. Esso vuole rappresentare, ospitando

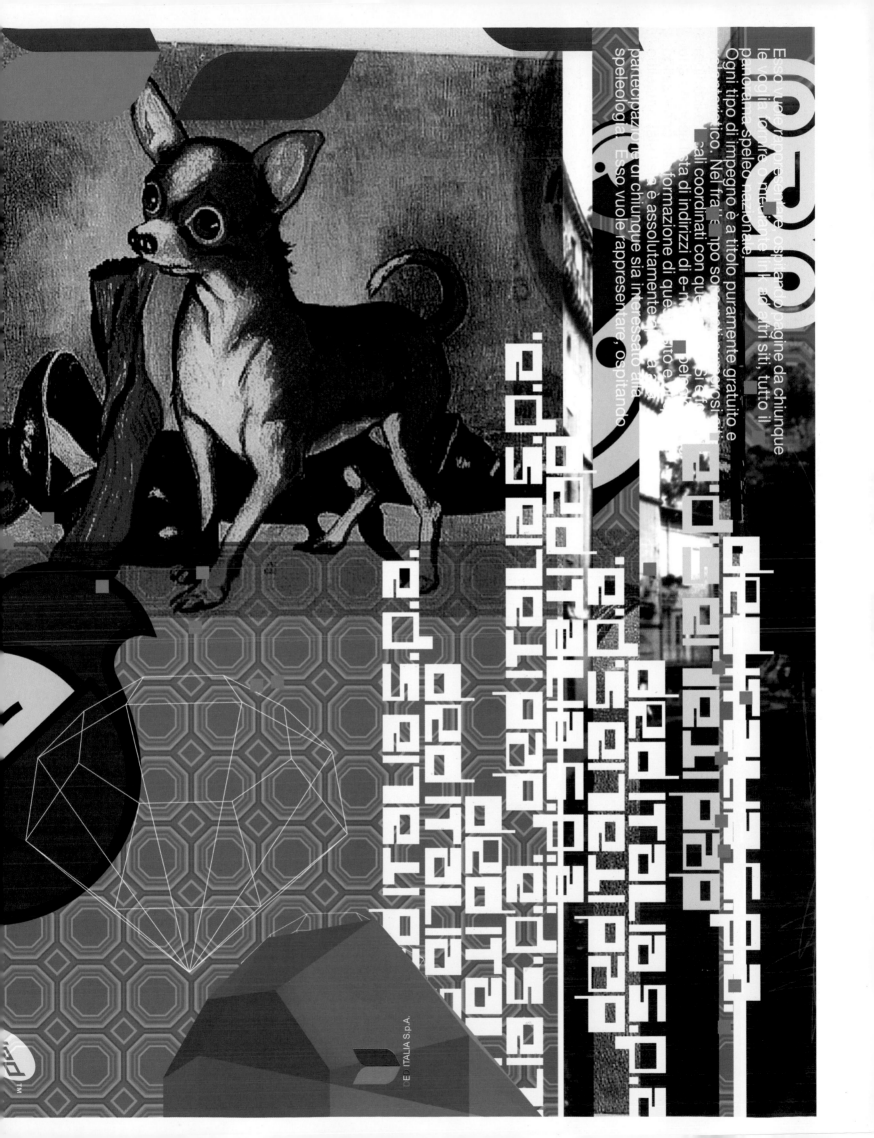

THE CREATURES
SAD CUNT

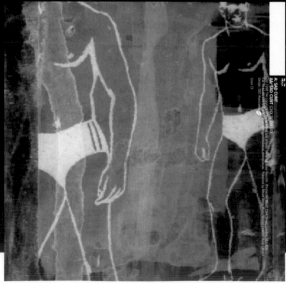

You'll be meeting with an intriguing business opportunity. A cattledrive that begins ea

CHANCE mihoko re

...will be happily resolved by nightfall. Your prospects are definitely on the upswing!

marok

INTRODUCING In Anbetracht der weltpolitischen Lage und der Tatsache, daß wieder deutsche Hurrapatrioten an vorderster Front kämpfen, haben wir uns schon mal in die Keller verzogen, um den pan-slawischen Bomben zu trotzen und weiterhin dem Trendsport zu fröhnen.

16

feldpost. contents of a sweet sixteen.
set in sound.
source direct, rootsmanuva, goodie mob, john coltrane...
photospecialactionfeature.
portfoley worldwide, ivory, tobin yelland, a.d. cam contemplates berlin, cristal movements by stadler, british columbia diaries...
artistic entertainmentfeatures.
stash, wohnseifer, the museum of barcelona, pact strikes again, too much coffee man, filmkredenzien zur berlinale, robert rodriguez, edward norton, nick king nolte, boba fettso, the miralanza factory...
fashionthrills for the people who fear fashinn.
hybernocular, ueberfahrene streetstyler, teeshirtdesign on a beautiful girl we forgot the name of, the crazy hairstyles of allen iverson...
material we can not classify.
henry fords vater und sein auto, ll's trendsportseite, the adventures of rock davis, billard lesson one, transmissions to the ldwnheadquarter...
the usual dumb shit.
sneakpreview, news and gadgets, editorial...
thank you for joining in.

Jeremy Klutz was ill this spring. he'll be back in no.17!
covershot. julian stranger by tobin yelland
introshot. jan waage by martin grüb

LODOWN
number one magazine for the moshpit renegades. hail satan.

No Skateboarding
=FUCK YOU= VK HATE

SDMC 84.12

crime. crime.

crime.

crime

For Safety's Sake

ON THIS
INC
PEDESTRIAN   AREAS

the new world plan rises from the underground

ADI Space-based Laser

Available to you
due to the lack of
competitors for Hegelian
Mastery of the Globe.

tract

ASS

WE MUST VENTURE
INTO THE UNKNOWN
DARKNESS.

"I arise in da mornin me and cut 2
fresh poop, put them old bruck
trainers on my foot, coz I'm da
actualistic, I max da most, drinking
Ginseng tea, eating hard-dough bread
toast." *Roots Manuva on "Sinking Sands"*

flexing some next type of motion shit...

DESIGN

AUSTRIA PRESENTS AUSTRIAN DESIGN IN THE CONTEXT OF A

DESIGN NOW.

ESENTS

ESIGN IN THE

AN

APPROACH

ES AND

USTRIA

RARY DESIGN.

P

W

ICO
TOD
CO
NEW
TEC
FAS
SLI
STA

ESIG

DESIGN NOW.AUSTRI

ARGENED APPROACH TO PURPOSES AND APPLICATIONS OF C

ICO
TO
CO
NE
TE
FA
SL
ST

S
Y
ES
RESOURCES
INOLOGIES
ION
ESHOWS
E AWARDS

DESIGN EXHIBITION

Always confronted with questions like these Sabotage Comm. presents the
20 20 Most Frequently Asked Questions, which should be understood as
service and help. The questions/answers were picked out of an
internal ask around and show the often asked Points, which should show
the background of Sabotage Comm. and get the right interpretation.
The 20 FAQ are a cross-selection of the Sabotage Comm. work and therefore
will not be answered anymore. Script and Photo can be used for public
purpose.

01. Since when does Sabotage exist
02. What was the first campaign
03. What's the reason Sabotage left the artbusiness
04. What does Sabotage want to reach or to change
05. What does Sabotage mean
06. Where and how does Sabotage act, which structure and tactic
07. What was the most spectacular act up to now
08. How would you categorize Sabotage
09. How many people are Sabotage
10. Since when does the label exist, and why actually music
11. What about music-sabotages
12. What's the label-philosophy and what's the feature of the label
13. Don't Sabotage get amused on the back of others
14. What does the Sabotage logo mean
15. Why has Sabotage got such a stylized graphic profile
16. How do the political activities of Sabotage look like
17. What's the forum of the Sabotage and is everyone a Saboteur
18. Does Sabotage follow a certain tradition
19. Are the main-subjects Sabotage pursued
20. How does the future look like for Sabotage

SABOTAGE COMMUNICATIONS presents 20 FA Q

Sabotage rec. 31   a division of SABOTAGE COMMUNICATIONS   Fax +43 1 218 31 55
E-mail sabotage@silverserver.co.at   www.bit-pilots.co.at/sabotage   visual attitudes: CH. STEINEGGER
photo by Oliver Ottenschläger

Made in Austria

Spieldauer:

№ ▬▬▬▬   Charakter:

Titel: 1.who wants to live forever 3:54
             2.somebo dy 3. 57   3.against all odds 3. 52
Komponist: 4.sea song 3.4 7   5.the power of love 5.2o
             6.nothing compares to 2 u 4.52
Eigentum: 7. hide and seek 5.1o   8.winter kills 4.56

Partitur	Piccolo	Hörner 1., 2., 3., 4.
Klavier-Auszug	1. Flöte	1. Trompete
Harmonium	2. Flöte	2. Trompete
1. Violinen	1. Oboe	3. Trompete
2. Violinen	2. Oboe	Tenorhorn 1., 2., 3.

BALLETT-STUDIO
JACK FLADUNG

		kl. Trommel
	2. Fagott	gr. Trommel
	Kontra-Fagott	Xylophon
	Saxophon I	Glockenspiel
	Saxophon II	Triangel
	Banjo	Div. Schlagzeug
Stimmen	Stimmen	Stimmen

»Súnova« Nr. 350a blau

NEW YORK STOCK EXCHANGE PRICES

4 pm close December 29

1997 High	Low	Stock	Div	Yld %	P/E	Sls 100s	High	Low	Close Quote	Ch'ge Prev. Close
[illegible]										

- A -

[illegible]

- C -

[illegible]

- F -

[illegible]

- J -

[illegible]

- K -

[illegible]

- P - Q -

[illegible]

- T -

[illegible]

- U -

[illegible]

- V -

[illegible]

- W -

[illegible]

- X - Y - Z -

[illegible]

[redacted]

Price data supplied by Extel, part of FT Information.

Yearly highs and lows for NYSE reflect the period from Jan 1 1997. Unless otherwise noted, rates of dividend are annual disbursements based on the latest declaration. Sales figures are unofficial.
... new yearly low. P/E price-earnings ratio. sls-sales. u-new yearly high. x-ex-dividend or ex-rights. yld-yield. z-sales in full.
... dealings suspended.

♣ FT Free Annual Reports Service

You can obtain the current annual reports and if available quarterly reports of any companies on the US exchanges with a ♣ symbol. To order reports ring (International Access) 1-804-320-8097 or give the names of the companies whose reports you want and fax your request to (International Access) 1-804-320-6135. Reports will be sent the next working day, subject to availability. You can also order online at http://www.icbinc.com/cgi-bin/ft5.

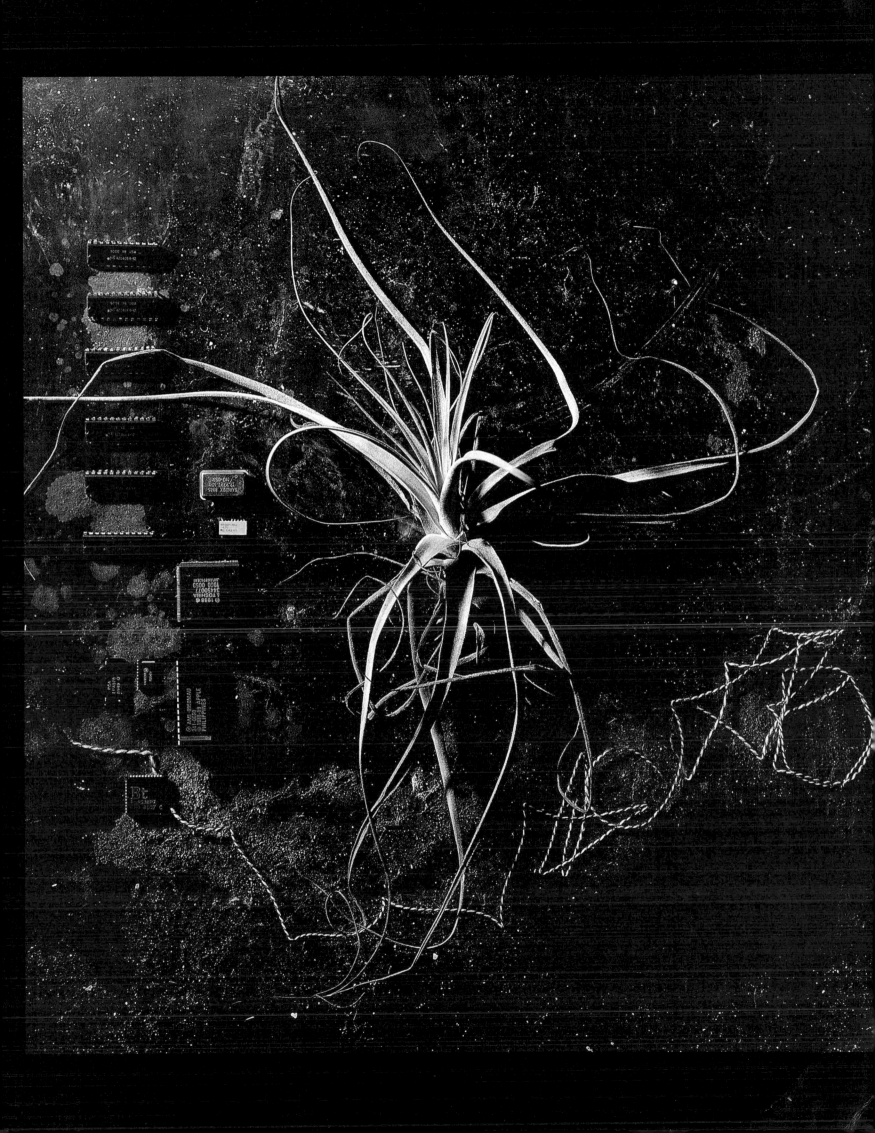

VIVA ZWEI ► Blockcodierungen 1/99

VIVA ZWEI ► Das Programm 1/99

PRO-PAIN The Truth Hur

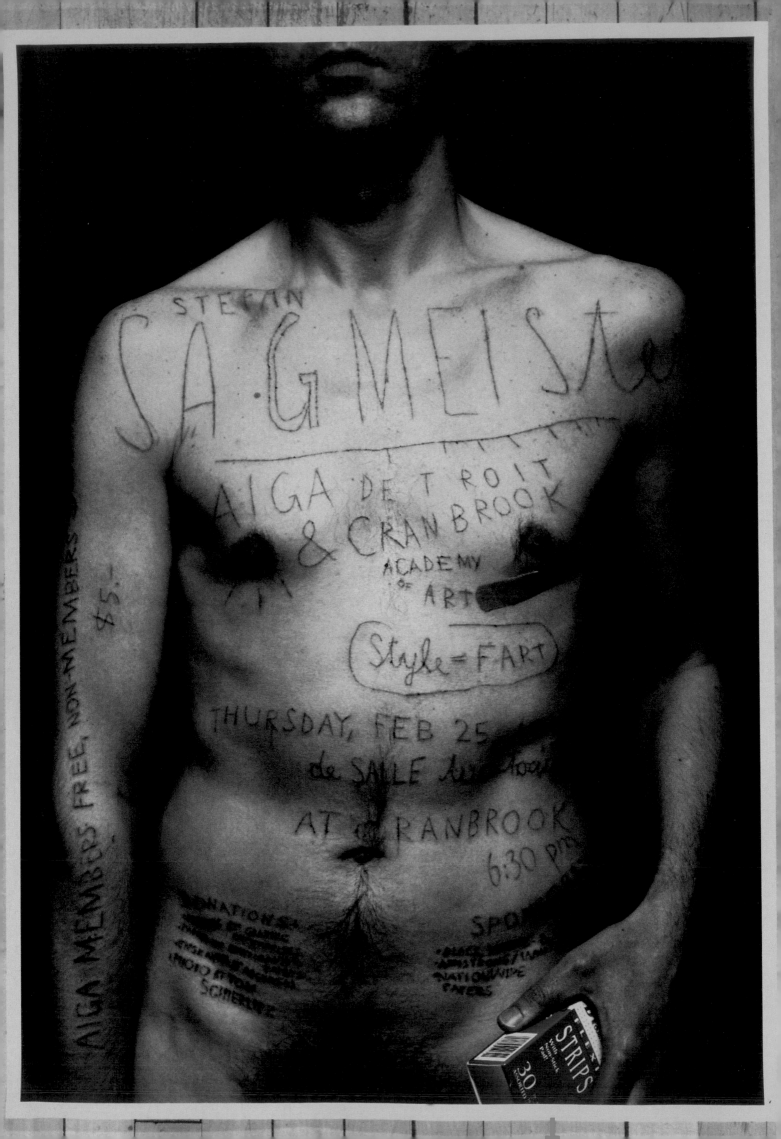

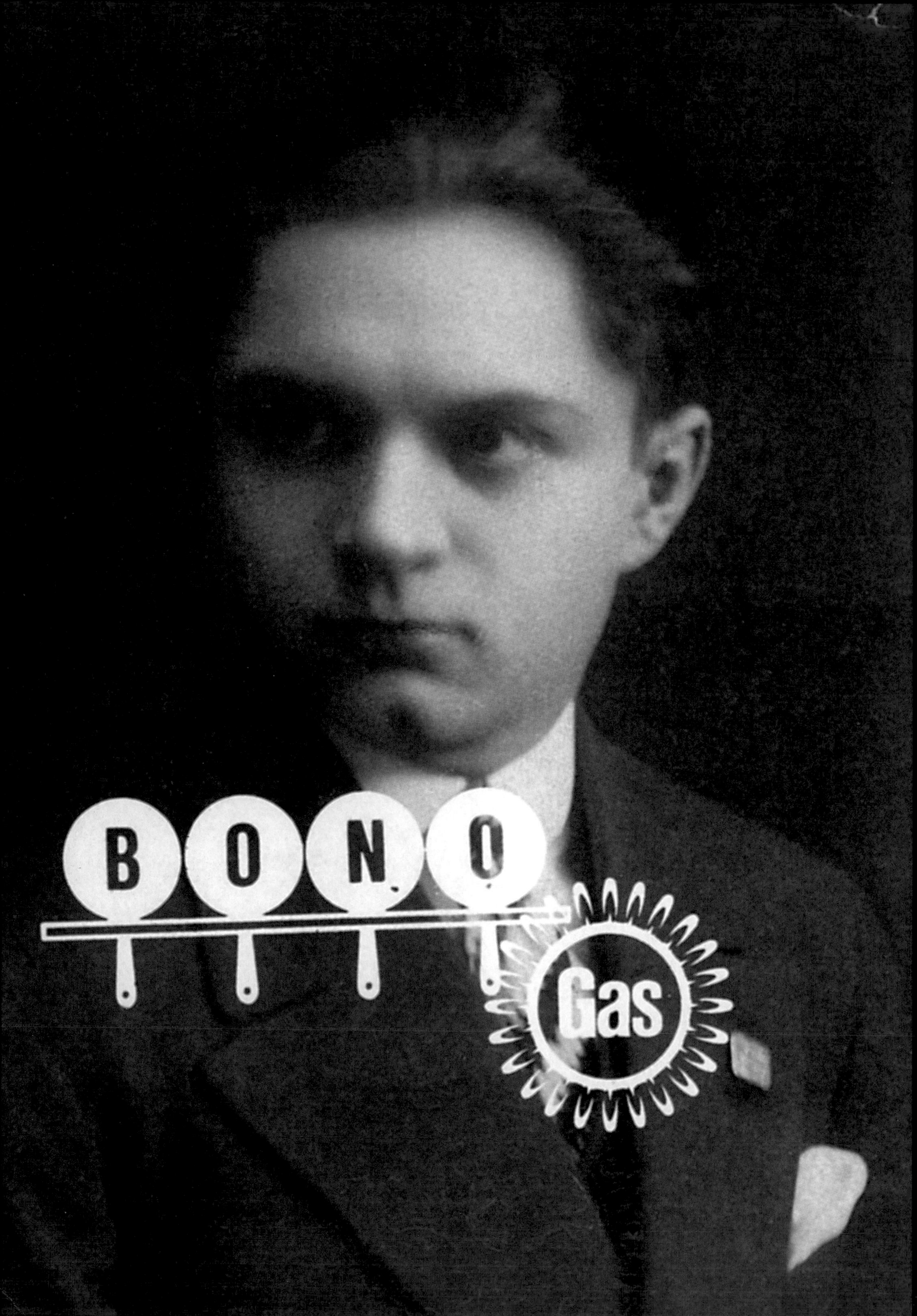
BONO
Gas

A DIVISION OF EMERSON ELECTRIC

MOTORPSYCHO
OZONE

[*ozone*]

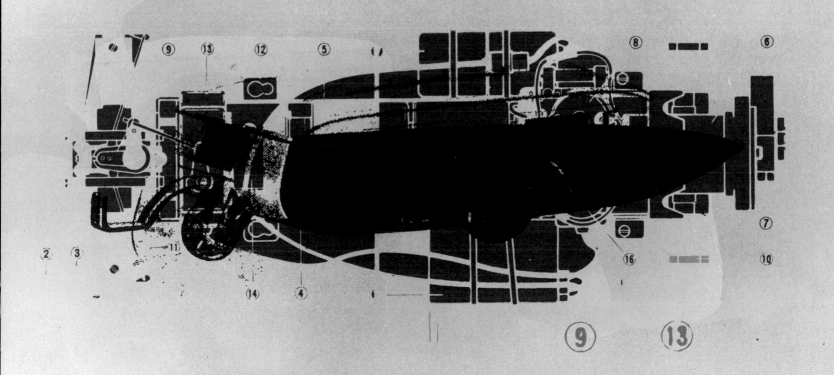

motorpsycho
TRUST US

recording information:

up our sleeves: athletic sound march 1997
wishing well : four track / athletic sound april 1997
flick of the wrist : athletic sound october 1996
instamatic : four track april 1997

starmelt / lovelight can also be found on our "angels and daemons at play" album,
but all else has not been previously released ever.

unproduced and fucked with by b.s. and deathprod.
engineers : he ge sten and kai e. andersen
mastered by craig morris at stripe audio
played and arranged by h. gebhardt, h.m. ryan and b. sæther

sleeve designed by kim hiorthøy

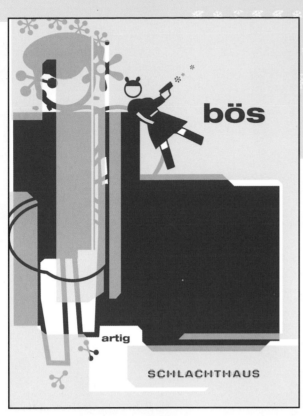

bös

artig

SCHLACHTHAUS

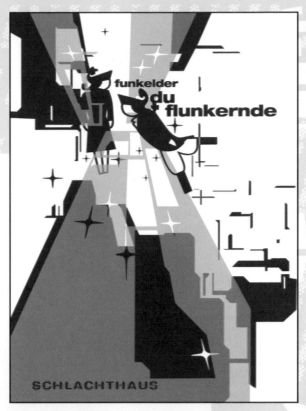

funkelder
du
flunkernde

SCHLACHTHAUS

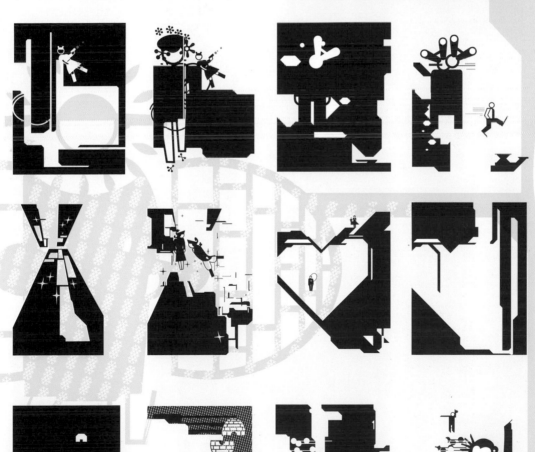

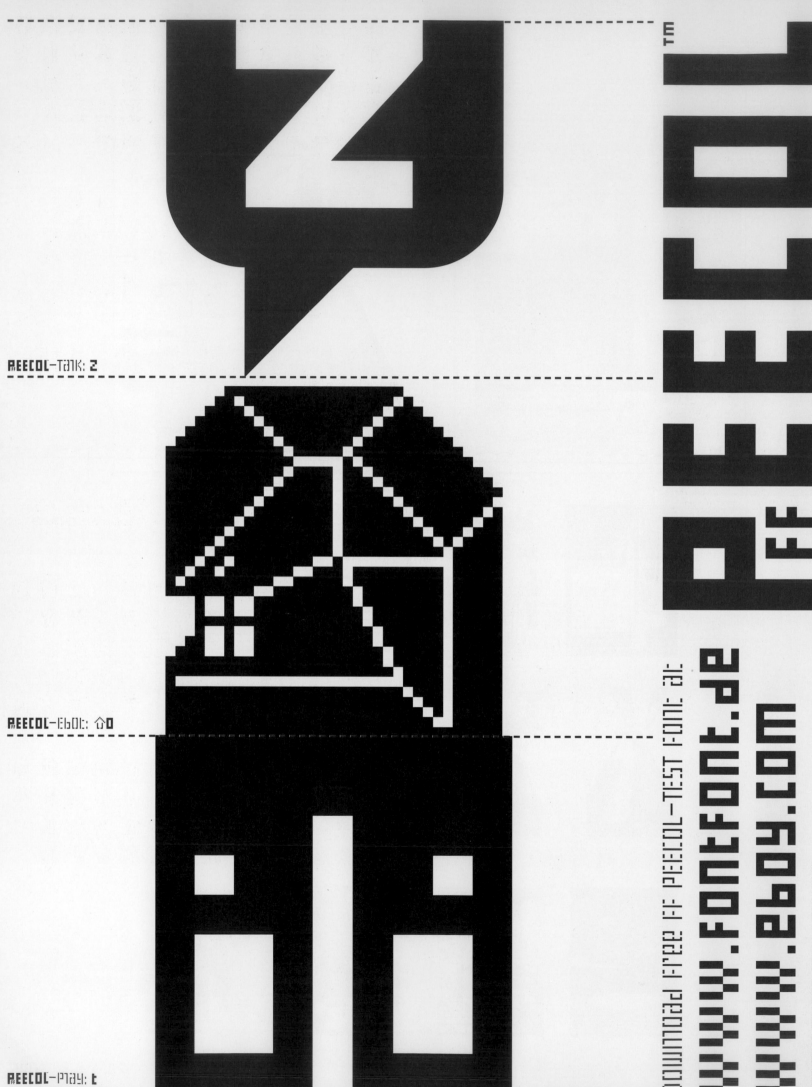

REECOL-TANK: Z

REECOL-EbOL: ⇧0

REECOL-PLAY: t

FF REECOL

™

FF-REECOL ©1998 EBOY-VERLAG, SAUERBREY - DISTRIBUTED BY FSI FONTSHOP INTERNATIONAL

FF-PEECOL-Ebot   FF-PEECOL-EbotPlus

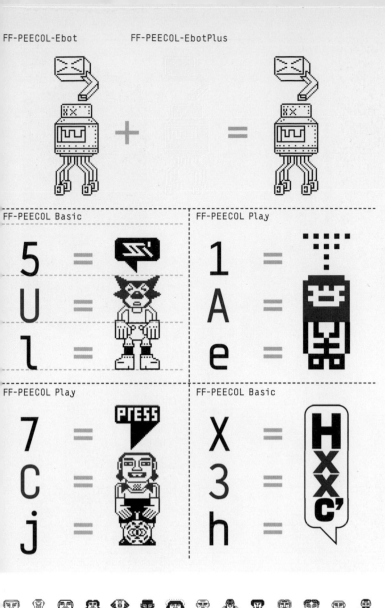

FF-PEECOL Basic

5 =
U =
l =

FF-PEECOL Play

1 =
A =
e =

FF-PEECOL Play

7 =
C =
J =

FF-PEECOL Basic

X =
3 =
h =

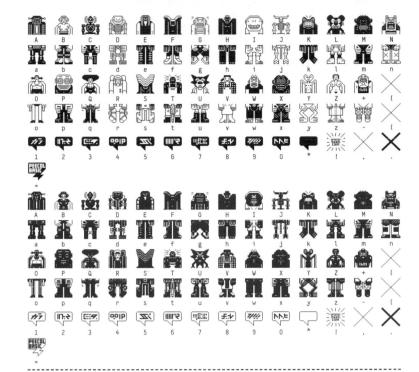

–Basic/–BasicPlus
FF PEECOL-Basic ©1998 eboy/kai vermehr

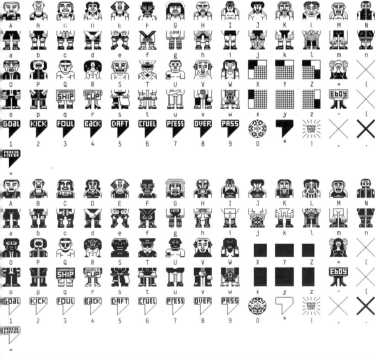

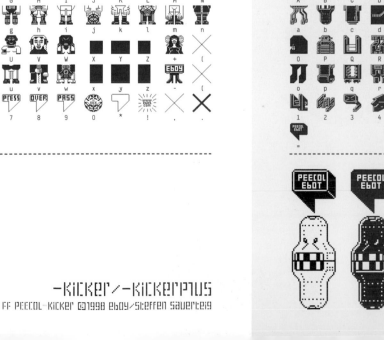

–Kicker/–KickerPlus
FF PEECOL-Kicker ©1998 eboy/steffen sauerteig

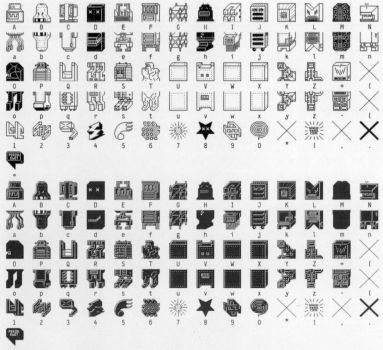

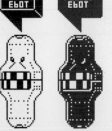

–Ebot/–EbotPlus
FF PEECOL-Ebot ©1998 eboy/kai vermehr

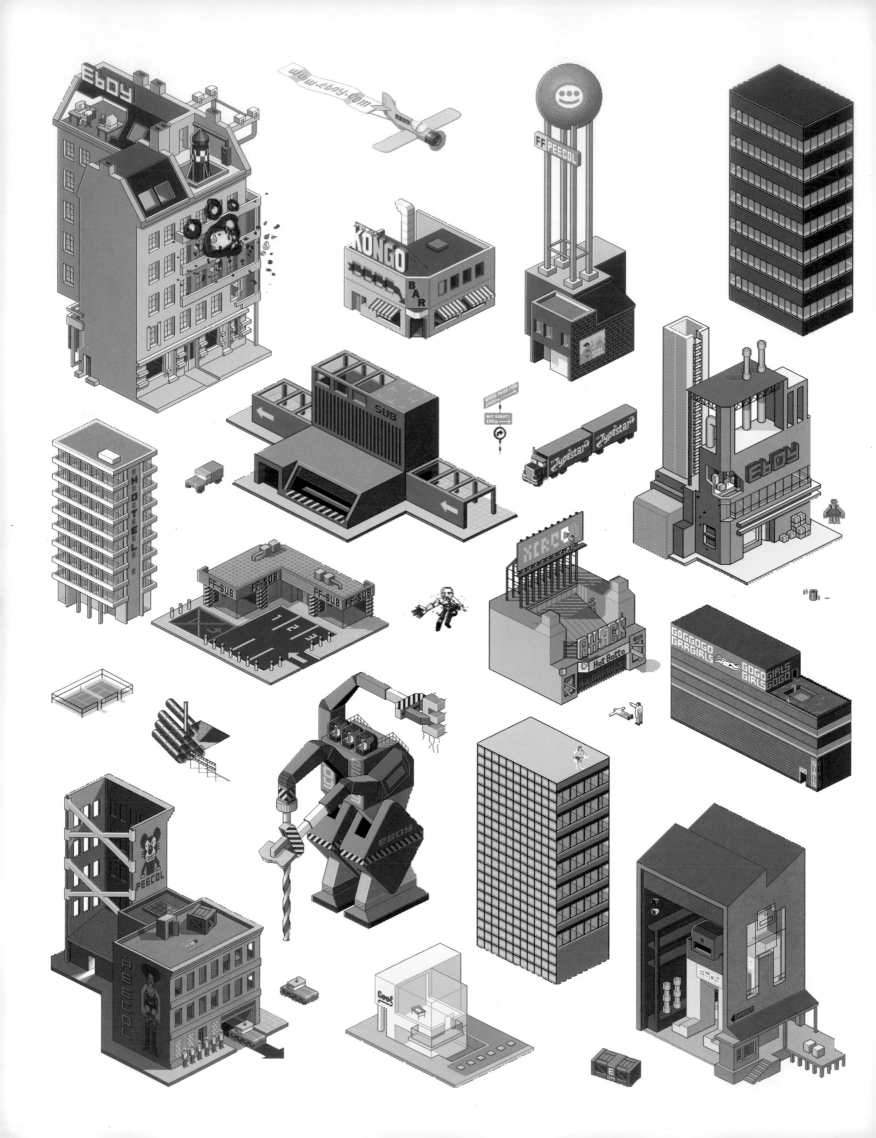

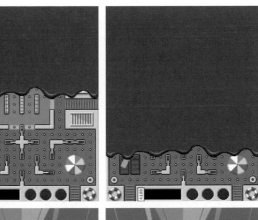
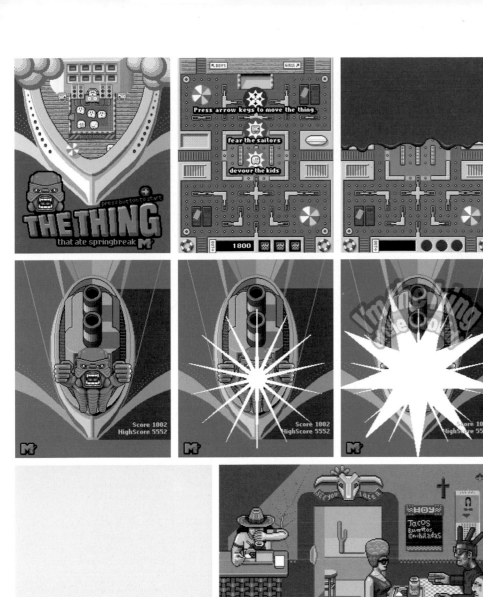

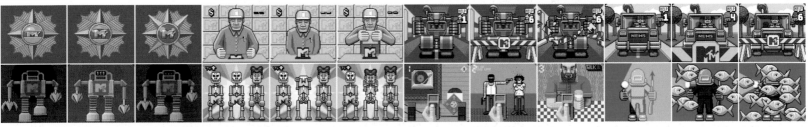
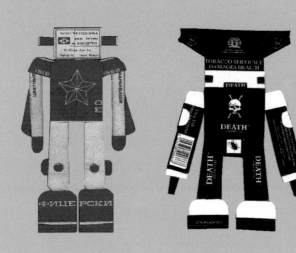
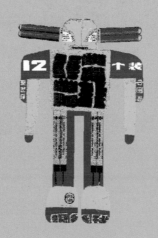

EbOY ▶ PEECOL SetS

SET AMBULANCE 01 @VERMEHR PEE COL@

★ REVOLUTION SET @STEFFEN SAUERTEIG EBOY PEECOL@

Game @STEFFEN

Game ◇ 02 @STEFFEN SAUERTEIG PEECOL@

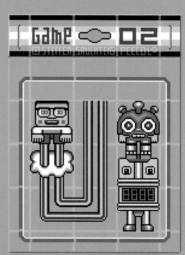

MR.P. VERMEHR 03

Game ◇ 01 @STEFFEN SAUERTEIG PEECOL@

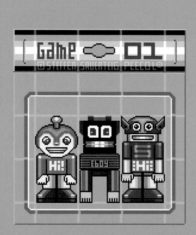

SET ACTION 02 @VERMEHR PEE COL@

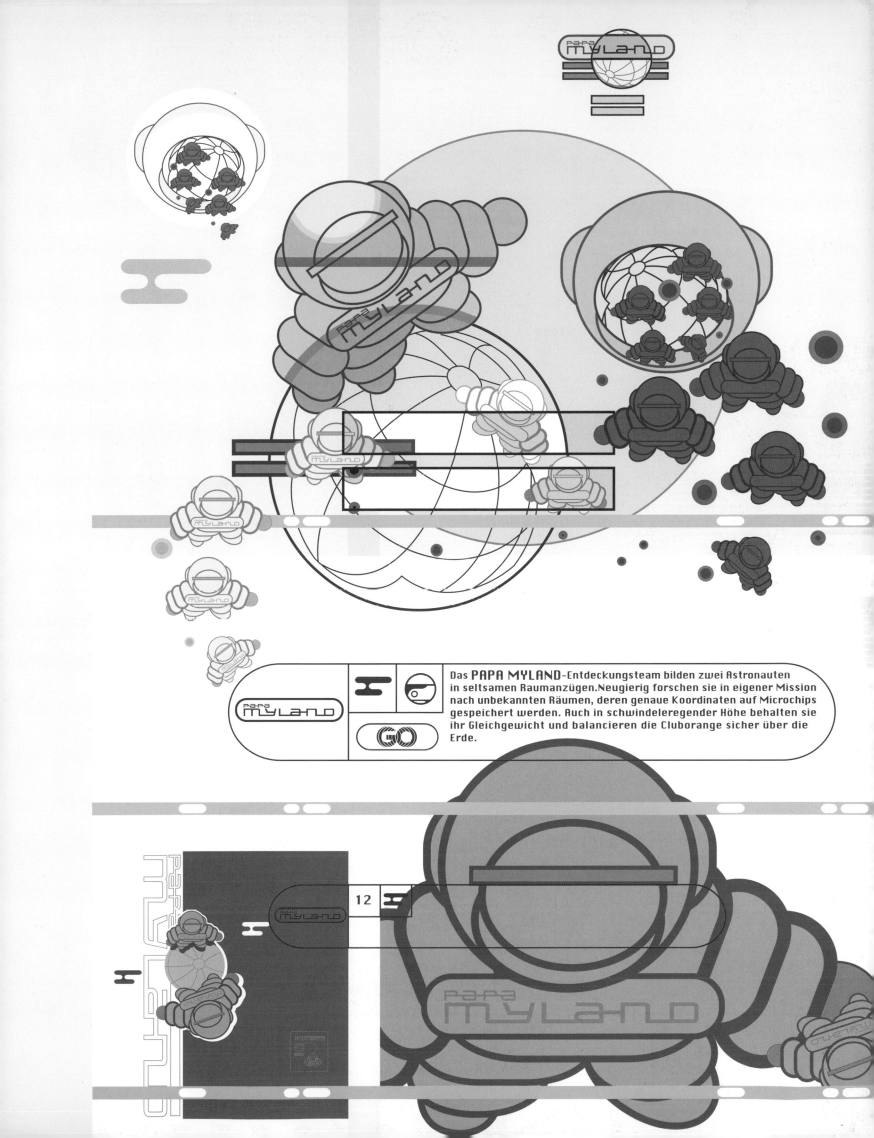

Das **PAPA MYLAND**-Entdeckungsteam bilden zwei Astronauten in seltsamen Raumanzügen.Neugierig forschen sie in eigener Mission nach unbekannten Räumen, deren genaue Koordinaten auf Microchips gespeichert werden. Auch in schwindeleregender Höhe behalten sie ihr Gleichgewicht und balancieren die Cluborange sicher über die Erde.

12

FRANCOIS CHALET
FRIEDBURGSTR. 5 8050 ZÜRICH
TELEFON 0041 079 241 818 83
HANDEL 0041 079 434 02 55
EMAIL CHALET@CHALETCOMP.CH

Tel. 033 223 38 86 · Türöffnung 22.00 Uhr · Gärt.98

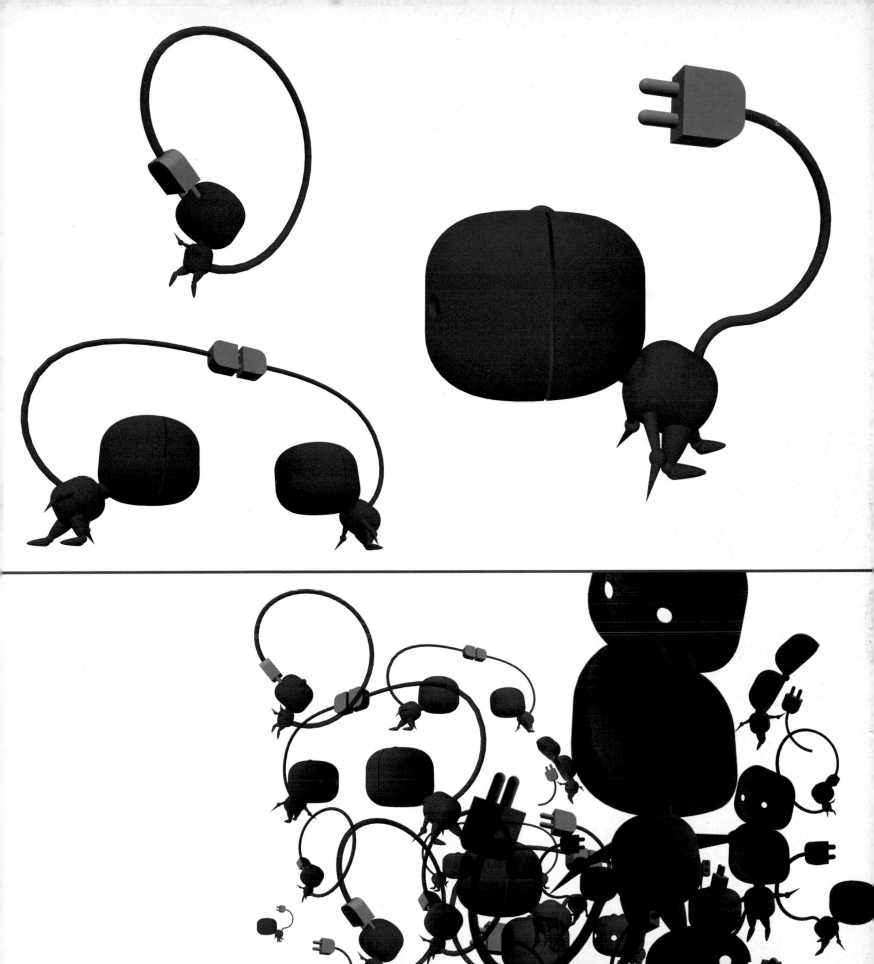

transit.

all tracks written and produced by sofa surfers
at monoscope audio room, vienna
mastered by oliver gross

10_t.2 lyrics by nanette dillard
03_s.3 containes the poem "anthem of a season"
by victor oshioke
12_a.1 soundscape + scratches by rob hdt
06_o.1 horns originally performed by oliver gross

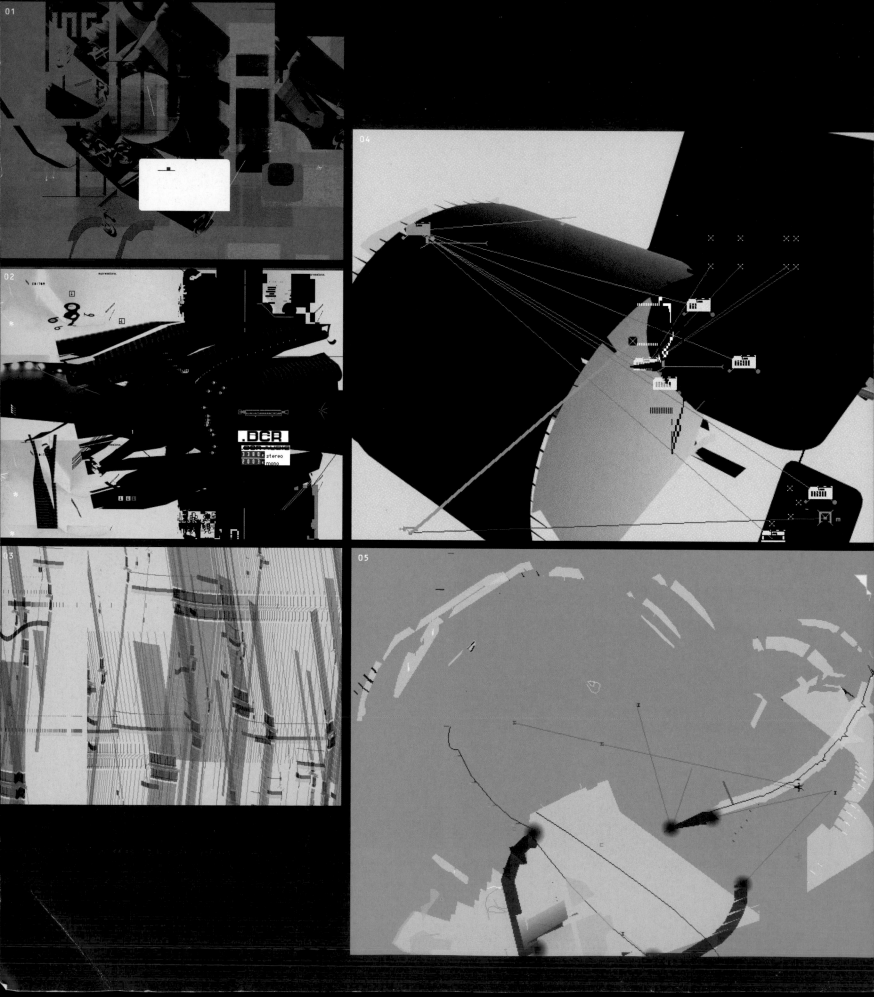

T/M

falling

from 1400 feet with an old friend.
the man beside her speaks.

"you are beautiful."

she thanks him, glances at me. we share a quiet
we step off the elev

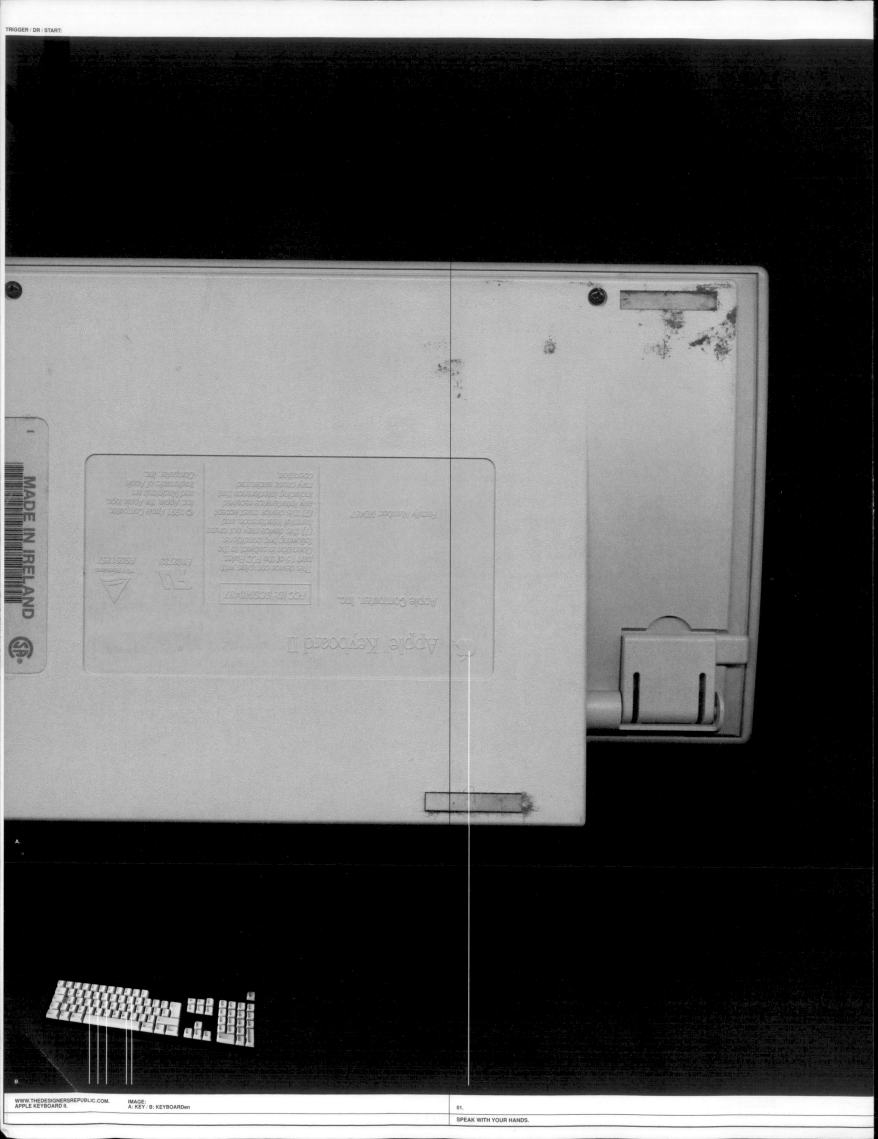

WWW.THEDESIGNERSREPUBLIC.COM.
APPLE KEYBOARD II.

IMAGE:
A: KEY / B: KEYBOARDen

01.

SPEAK WITH YOUR HANDS.

14 FOR SHEFFIELD.
00Y 0K.

IMAGE:
C: MA 8 RUN / D: 0C 0M 100Y 0K

02.

DIRECTION.

E.

ENGLISH IS THE NEW JAPANESE.
DAT TAPE BUILD.

IMAGE:
E: DAT TOP.2 / DAT SIDE.2 / DAT OPEN.2 / DAT SIDE

03.

MOVEMENT.

STRUCTION FOR USE.
IN?

IMAGE:
F: GARAGE PAY

04.

SPEED.

NO
BALL PLAYING OFF
THIS WALL OR
SKATEBOARDING
ALLOWED

= SIX FEET.

EXPOSED
MACROMEDIA STICKER BACK

IMAGE:
G: HOP SCOTCH / H: CONCRETE / I: NO.

05.

SCALE.

Fragile
Furniture

C+S
P.O.#29296-5

CAUTION
IF CARTON IS TORN OR CRUSHED, INSPECT FOR CONCEALED DAMAGE
AND FILE CLAIM WITH DELIVERING CARRIER WITHIN 15 DAY LIMIT.

ABOUT DAMAGED SHIPMENTS

1. If these goods are damaged in transit the DELIVERING TRANSPORTA-
   TION COMPANY is required by law to make solution of damage on your
   paid freight bill.
2. It is only claims that may be CONCEALED damage, they are obliged to make
   inspection AFTER goods after inspection.
3. Transportation rates are made in proportion to value of merchandise moving, therefore the Carrier
   will not pay of loss should be made in proportion to such value as to their, ordinary retires you all
   be filed with the delivering transportation carrier.

● PLEASE DO NOT RETURN GOODS TO US
  WITHOUT CARE SHIPPING INSTRUCTIONS

This Side Up

NWICH VILLAGE, NYC. IMAGES:
J: MANCHESTER DEPARTURE / K: JET INTAKE / L: BOXED / M: DANGER.   INSTRUCTIONS.   06.

THE CORRECT USE OF AN ARROW.

BUILDING.
PERSPECTIVE FORCED.

IMAGE:
N: CASA U: GROUND FLOOR MEZZANINE.

TECTONIC-TURE.

MAGE AREA:
235 X 279MM.
CMYK.

STOP.

SION.
EASUREMENTS ARE IN MILLIMETRES.   IMAGE:
O: N/A.

FONT USED THROUGHOUT:
SYSTEM HELVETICA.

08.

MEASUREMENT.

52 mm
info@52mm.com >> www.52mm.com

aeonflux | autobulb d.care >> Jan Rikus Hillmann
aeonflux@de-bug.de

Andreas Prossliner
Phone: +49-177-478 11 62

Bastien Aubry for Silex
baubry@eclat.ch

Approach & Identity >> N
clear@rocketmail.com

Chalet >> François Chalet
chalet@datacomm.ch >> www.francoischalet.ch

DED Associates >> Nik + Jon Daughtry
ded@dedass.com >> www.dedass.com

D. Martijn Oostra

e-boy
eboy@eboy.com >> www.eboy.com

Formgeber >> Robin Pastyr
pastyr@formgeber.de >> www.formgeber.de

Function
function@function.org >> www.function.org

G >> Peter Gärtl
gärtl@hotmail.com

Hell
henni@die-gestalten.de

      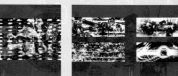

Judith Rüegger, Anna Albisetti
ausdemhause@losamigos.ch

Kai Twellbeck (Stuttgart)

Kim Hiorthoy
kimim@online.no

Marc Kappeler
mkappeler@access.ch

Marok
lodown@lodown.de >> www.lodown.de

Martin Woodtli
martinwoodtli@hotmail.com

Pfadfinderei.Mitte >> Critzla, Honza
critzla@snafu.de

Planet Pixel
planetpixel@netcologne.de >> www.planetpixel.de

Ruth Held
bildwurf@dial.eunet.ch

Sagmeister Inc. >> Stefan Sagmeister
ssagmeiste@aol.com

Speedshop Graphics
P.O.Box 361, FIN-00121 Helsinki

Surface >> Markus Weisbeck
weisbeck@surface.de >> www.surface.de

Sweden
hello@swedengraphics.com >> www.swedengraphics.com

Toursalon >> Katrin Wiens - Kristina Teubner
toursalon@compuserve.com

Transport
www.sfgl.ch/transport

Tycoon Graphics
mail@tyg.co.jp >> www.towatei.com/tyg/

Ukawa Naohiro > MoM'n'DaD Productions
momndad@coconet.ne.jp

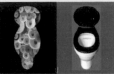 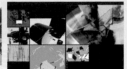   

anca Strauch
ancastrauch@gmx.net

BOROS • Agentur für Kommunikation
>> Ingo Maak > maak@boros.de

büro destruct
bd@bermuda.ch >> www.bermuda.ch/bureaudestruct

Büro X >> Christoph Steinegger / Guenter Eder
cs@buerox.de >> www.buerox.de

Dextro
dextro@dextro.org >> www.dextro.org / www.turux.org

Dirk Rudolph
dirk@rudolph.bo.uunet.de >> www.dirkrudolph.de

    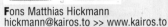

Eikes Grafischer Hort
hort@bigfoot.com >> www.eikesgrafischerhort.com

Factor Product >> Stefan Bogner
contact@factor-product.com >> www.factor-product.com

Fons Matthias Hickmann
hickmann@kairos.to >> www.kairos.to

Hideki Inaba Design >> Hideki Inaba
inaba@t3.rim.or.jp

HinderSchlatterFeuz Grafik
hinderschlatterfeuz@bluewin.ch

i_d büro GmbH >> Krimmel/Osterwalder
i_dbuero@compuserve.com >> www.janglednerves.com/i_dbuero

Johannes Deutsch
www.johannes-deutsch.at

 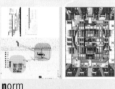  

King Cay Lab >> Toshiaki Uchikoshi
kingcay@sepia.ocn.ne.jp

KM7
klaus.mai@frankfurt.netsurf.de >> www.km7.de

Maja Gusberti
maia@re-p.at >> www.re-p.at

ka Mischler
ka@die-gestalten.de

norm
md.norm@datacomm.ch

O/R/E/L > Abuse Industries > Andy Orel
mona@sin.at

Production 13 >> David Zack Custer Freelance / Positive±Negative
production13@hotmail.com

Stefan Gandl
stefan@designerdock.de

(**S**trada
strada@x3network.net

Stylorouge >> Rob O'Connor
stylo@easynet.co.uk >> www.stylorouge.co.uk

he Designers Republic
@thedesignersrepublic.com >> www.thedesignersrepublic.com

Threshold House >> Peter Christopherson / John Balance
john@loci.demon.co.uk >> www.brainwashed.com/coil

United Visions >> Sascha Lüönd
sascha.lueoend@frankfurt.netsurf.de

Weissraum >> Brück, Buchholz, Kielzer
weissraum@provi.de

Wieden & Kennedy Amsterdam
Nike > Frank Striefler

Die Deutsche Bibliothek-
CIP Einheitsaufnahme

Klanten, Robert:
Trigger/Hrsg.:
Robert Klanten,
Hendrik Hellige,
Michael Mischler-
Berlin: Die- Gestalten- Ver., dgv, 1999
ISBN 3- 931126-21-8

Trigger

edited by Robert Klanten,
Hendrik Hellige,
Michael Mischler

printed by Medialis Offset, Berlin
Made in Europe

dgv- Die Gestalten Verlag , Berlin
Fax: +49. 30. 30871068
Email: verlag@die-gestalten.de
www.die-gestalten.de

Distributed/ represented through:

USA / Canada:

Consortium BSD
1045 Westgate Drive
St. Paul
Minnesota 55114/ 1065
Tel: +1. 651. 221 90 35
Fax: +1. 651. 917 64 06
Email: mail@cbsd.com

Great Britain / Ireland / Asia/ Scandinavia:

Art Books International
1 Steward´s Court 220 Steward´s Rd
London SW 8 4UD
Tel: +44. 171. 720 15 03
Fax: +44. 171. 720 31 58
Email: mail@art-bks.com

Japan:

Infinite Books
1-25-2 Nishihara, Shibuya-ku
Tokyo
Tel: +81. 3. 346 95708
Fax: +81. 3. 346 95708

Deutschland:

LKG
Pötschauer Weg
D - 04579 Espenhain
Tel: +49 34206 65121
Fax: +49 34206 65110

In case you should have problems
finding our books in your country,
please contact dgv directly or
look up our website.

BLAG
Sally and Sarah Edwards
160 pages, 24.4 x 30.5 cm
full colour, approx. 200 photos, Softcover
DM 69 £ 24.99 $ 39.99 ••• ISBN 3-931126-31-5
release: September '99

SPARK
by Dirk Rudolph
160 pages, 24 x 28 cm
full colour, approx. 200 illustrations, Softcover
DM 69 £ 24.99 $ 39.99 ••• ISBN 3-931126-33-1
release: September '99

POP TICS
by Bungalow Records
H. Beier, M. Liesenfeld / Bungalow
40 pages, 15 x 15 cm,
special see-through box, including free audio CD
DM 29.90 £ 12.99 $ 19.99 ••• ISBN 3-931126-30-7
release: November '99

SPACE MANUAL
by Anja Osterwalder
41 pages, 24 x 33 cm
full colour, approx. 40 photos, special vacuum packaging,
rounded edges, O-wire binding
vollfarbig, ca. 40 Fotos, Vakuum-Sonderverpackung,
abgerundete Ecken, Kalenderbindung
english version: £ 26.99 $ 39.99 ••• ISBN 3-931126-26-9
deutsche Ausgabe: DM 69 ••• ISBN 3-931126-28-5
release: August '99

Büro Destruct
Büro Destruct
192 pages, 24 x 28 cm
5-special colour print, Softcover
DM 69 $ 44 £ 27,99 ••• ISBN 3-931126-24-2

BUSY
by Jim Avignon & DAG
160 pages, 24 x 28 cm
full colour, approx. 200 illustrations,
in English / German, Softcover
vollfarbig, ca. 200 Illustrationen,
in Englisch / Deutsch, Paperback
DM 59 £ 24.99 $ 38.99 ••• ISBN 3-931126-17-X

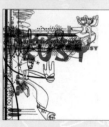

DESIGN AGENT KM7 - LICENCE TO DESIGN
by Klaus Mai / Louis Flanigan
152 pages, 24 x 28 cm
5-colour print, Softcover
DM 59 £ 24.99 $ 34.99 ••• ISBN 3-931126-14-5

LODOWN - GRAPHIC ENGINEERING
by Marok
Thomas Marecki a.k.a. Marok
176 pages, 29 x 22 cm,
landscape format, full colour, Softcover
DM 59 £ 24.99 $ 39.99 ••• ISBN 3-931126-16-1

FLYERMANIA
Die Gestalten
96 pages, 15 x 21,5 cm
Softcover
£ 9.99 $ 14.99 ••• ISBN 3-931126-15-3

only available through dgv
outside D / A / CH